Sail Better

Also by Roger Marshall

Marshall's Marine Sourcebook
Designed to Cruise
Yacht Design Details
A Sailor's Guide to Production Sailboats
Designed to Win
Race to Win

Sail Better

101 TIPS AND TECHNIQUES

ROGER MARSHALL

ST. MARTIN'S GRIFFIN NEW YORK

Design by Bonni Leon Berman

Library of Congress Cataloging-in-Publication Data

Marshall, Roger.
   Sail better : 101 tips and techniques / Roger Marshall.—1st ed.
     p.   cm.
     Includes index.
   ISBN 0-312-14133-5
     1. Sailing. 2. Yachts and yachting. I. Title.
   GV811.M26 1996
   797.1'24—dc20   95-36249
                                               CIP

First Edition: April 1996

10 9 8 7 6 5 4 3 2 1

Contents

PART TWO: PERFORMANCE SAILING 123

Introduction

Several years ago, the editor of the local newspaper approached me about writing short articles showing readers how to sail better. The tips and techniques in these articles formed the basis for this book. Since their initial appearance, each idea has been carefully analyzed and updated in light of modern techniques.

As a yacht designer, I have always been interested in ways to make a boat sail faster and handle easier. As I grow older, faster translates into more comfortable, and handling better translates into making the work load smaller. Speed is not the overriding factor it once was, but speed is still important in many ways. For example, sailing your boat faster can get you into harbor before a storm hits, rather than being several miles from harbor in rain and high winds.

The ideas that follow are intended to be read in short sessions, not as a long story on how to improve your sailing style. Each idea represents the fruit of many miles at sea, under sun, rain, and stars, and with many different crews. Bless 'em all. Often, the ideas have been debated ferociously around a draught of ale, with viewpoints drawn on the tablecloth. These tips or techniques have stood the test of time and served most users well. I hope they will do so for you.

If you disagree with my ideas or have something to add, I'd love to hear from you. It is only by testing ideas and adding your thoughts and experience to that of other sailors that techniques and tips spread and improve. I can't promise to reply to your letter, however—I may well be off sailing.

—ROGER MARSHALL
Sail Better
c/o St. Martin's Press
175 Fifth Avenue
New York, NY 10010-7848

PART ONE

CRUISING

Sailing with Children

It's summer and you want to go sailing, but someone in your family needs to do some shopping and someone else wants to play ball. It seems as if the expensive boat you bought last year will sit on its mooring for another weekend. Why does your family always seem to make excuses to avoid a sailing trip? Maybe it's because you yelled at your daughter when she stepped into the bight of the mainsheet, or because you lost your temper when your son spilled his fruit juice on a bunk.

Disasters happen. At sea, kids step in the wrong spot and can easily get in the way. It requires a certain amount of planning and organization to take children sailing. In the following pages we'll look at how to get the entire family to enjoy sailing together.

First, we'll consider child-proofing your yacht. Then we'll look at essential safety features. We'll follow with things to keep children occupied during a sailing trip. And finally, we'll look at how the whole family can have fun, not only at your destination, but also going there and getting back.

1: Child-Proofing a Boat

What is the most expensive equipment on your boat? Probably the electronics in the navigation area. Should you therefore put your navigation area off limits to children? This may be your first reaction, but there are many things your children can enjoy doing at the nav table. How can you keep your electronic gear safe while allowing the kids to have a good time?

One easy step is to cover the faces of your electronic gear with pieces of clear plastic that have holes cut out for the knobs. If you don't mind retuning your instruments, you can then let your children turn the knobs all they want. Even a simple plastic bag held in place by an elastic band will stop sticky fingers from gumming up the equipment while allowing them to turn the dials.

Another sheet of clear plastic or acrylic (Lexcan or Plexiglass in the U.S. and Perspex in the U.K.) will allow you to display the chart on the navigation table while protecting it from crayons and other hazards imposed by small fingers. You can also plot your course on the plastic by writing on it with a grease pencil. (Another option is to cover each chart with clear plastic laminate.) The drawers of the navigation table should have catches on them that are hard for small hands to open but which allow easy access to larger hands. You can purchase childproof catches for your home at any hardware store. For your boat, try to get corrosion-resistant catches.

In the galley, the stove is the biggest danger. Not only is it hot, it is also gimballed and easy to tip over. Most boat stoves also use a heavier-than-air, flammable gas. Given these hazards, it is wise to keep the area near the stove off limits. Also make sure that, whenever it is not in use, you turn the stove off at the gas line and at the tank in the cockpit locker. And keep matches or the stove lighter, as well as the gas line control knob, out of children's reach.

Knives are the next worst hazard in the galley. If you have already made the stove off limits, consider installing a knife rack behind the stove. This area would then become part of the off-limits space. If your galley has a tiled floor, cover it with cork or a rubber mat to prevent serious injuries. Many sailors have sections of carpet or canvas they lay down when the boat is in port, both to protect the sole and to prevent slipping. If you have a highly polished, varnished cabin sole, it can be very treacherous even to adults, so you might want to sprinkle sand or some form of non-skid material on it when you next varnish.

Bunks don't require much protection if you cover them. A cotton-backed plastic material is your best choice: it is easy to clean and repels dirt.

All bunks should have leecloths. Many children roll around when they sleep, and a leecloth will keep them in the bunk in almost all conditions. Figure 1-1 shows how a leecloth should be fitted.

In the head compartment, the toilet must be off limits for play. The last thing you'll want to do on a Sunday afternoon is dismantle the head to get a child's favorite toy out while the child stands by, crying loudly. Also make sure that the head door can

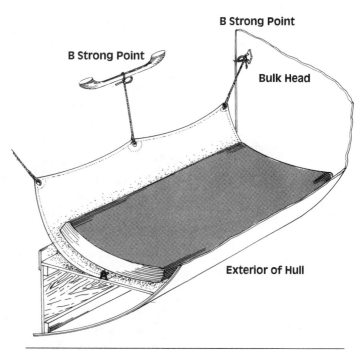

Figure 1-1: A leecloth can be used to keep small children securely in their bunks. The leecloth should be screwed to the bunk flat (A) so that it can be stowed under the cushion and can be used to make the bunk cushion more horizontal, if required. Note also the strong points (B) to which the leeboard is tied. They should be well out of a child's reach.

be opened easily from both sides by someone who is three feet tall. For a small child, being locked in a tiny compartment can be quite traumatic.

The companionway ladder can be a site of many accidents. To help prevent children from falling there, glue non-skid material to every rung and cut handholds low enough in the sides of the ladder for children to reach. Additional handholds should be added for very small children. You might also want to cut lengthwise slots in the ladder rungs as shown in Figure 1-2. Children going up and down a ladder are more likely to hold onto the rung than the side, and a rung that allows the child to get a grip on it is easier and safer for climbing.

Handholds in the remainder of the interior are usually too high for children. Watch your children as they walk through the boat and install additional handrails at their level where they may be needed.

Once you have child-proofed your boat as best you can, let your children

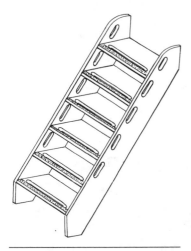

roam. You can then devise more ways of preventing accidents if you watch to see where they get into trouble.

2: Life Jackets

Life jackets should be worn on deck by all children when under sail, no matter how well they swim. The only exception is when the child is wearing a strong harness, properly tethered to the center of the boat, and safety nettings are firmly secured all around the lifelines. Children under the age of six should wear life jackets on deck and at dockside at *all* times; no exceptions. You may want to have this same rule for all children who cannot swim, regardless of their age. Use your own best judgment.

Figure 1-2: Slots or grooves about ¾" wide cut in the tread of the companionway ladder make it easier for a young child to climb up and down. Handholds cut low down on the sides also make it easier for the child to move around below deck.

In America life jackets must meet U.S. Coast Guard Standards. In Britain and Europe they should meet Comité Européan de Normalisation (CEN) Standards (see Appendix A). Make sure that your children's life jackets fit properly and fasten securely; some children can outgrow a jacket during a single season. When replacing a life jacket, check to see that it will support the weight of the child until the child grows out of it.

As a general rule, it is better to buy a larger size that will accommodate your child's growth, as long as the child can wear it comfortably and securely.

3: Harnesses

A harness will give children who do not swim confidence on a boat, and will also give parents the security of knowing that the child cannot accidentally fall into the water. Few harnesses are available for small children, however. One exception is the Lirakis harness shown in Figure 3-1. (See Appendix B for the names and addresses of manufacturers of safety equipment.) This harness is designed to suit children between the ages of 18 months and 4 years. It can be worn frontwards as well as backwards to enable parents to hold onto the safety hook when walking down the dock or to watch children without holding the harness.

If you intend to secure your child with a harness, make sure you have a strongly bolted padeye in a position that gives the child plenty of room to play. The bottom or side of the cockpit is one recommended position; the line should be long enough for the child to sit comfortably on the cockpit seat, see over the side, or play in the cockpit. Another idea is to use a jackline, or jackstay, to allow the child to roam around the boat. The line should run from the cockpit side deck to the foredeck without passing under major obstructions. It should be strong enough to also support the weight of an adult who might clip on in inclement conditions. Most lines have a padeye at both ends and a ¼" (6mm) wire shackled to the padeyes.

Figure 3-1: The Lirakis child harness can be worn frontwards as well as backwards.

4: Safety Netting

Safety netting gives parents an extra measure of security when sailing with children. Safety netting can be secured inside the lifelines from the bow to the stern. The best type of netting is one with a mesh size of less than two inches that will support about a hundred pounds. Netting can be made of nylon or cotton and should be strongly secured at the top of the lifelines and at the toerail. If your boat does not have an alloy toerail, secure the netting between the lifeline stanchions with either a third lifeline wire threaded through the stanchion bases or with small padeyes through-bolted to the toerail or deck. Since most stanchions are positioned at a maximum of seven feet from one another, use at least two padeyes between stanchions.

When effectively installed around the boat, a strong netting will support the weight of an adult falling against it and the weight of sails that are tied on the foredeck. Netting should not be used as a substitute for a harness or life jacket, however. Stanchions are usually only twenty-four or twenty-seven inches high, and an adventurous child can climb over them.

5: Bunkboards and Leecloths

Infants can usually sleep aboard a boat in a travel bed securely fitted in a bunk with a strong leecloth, but it isn't long before children outgrow this arrangement. Older children want a place of their own with room for their toys and stuffed animals. They also need a bunk they can roll around in without falling out. This makes a leeboard or leecloth essential. Figure 1-1 shows a leecloth and Figure 5-1 shows a leeboard fabricated from ¼" or ⅜" plywood. (Use the thicker wood for larger children.)

In Figure 5-1 the plywood bunkboard (B) folds down for storage under the mattress when not in use, and strong catches hooked into padeyes, or barrel bolts lock it in place. This board can be adjusted by fitting two or three sets of padeyes, or drilling two or three sets of holes for the barrel bolts, as shown in Figure 5-2. To make the board more interesting for the child, drill it with holes, cut holes of different shapes, paint the inside, or cover it with cut-out cartoon figures. The holes should not be large enough to provide a toehold for the child to climb out. Another option is to add a large drop-in or hinged piece to the leeboard, with a hole cut in the middle, that divides the bunk into two parts. A child will often play for hours with an arrangement like the one shown in Figure 5-3.

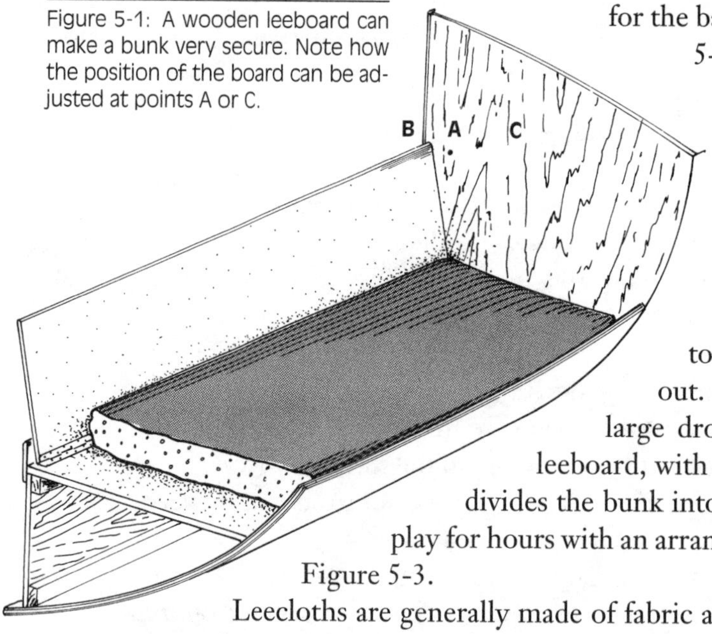

Figure 5-1: A wooden leeboard can make a bunk very secure. Note how the position of the board can be adjusted at points A or C.

Leecloths are generally made of fabric and are stored under the mattress when not in use. Leecloths work well for kids, but remember to tie the

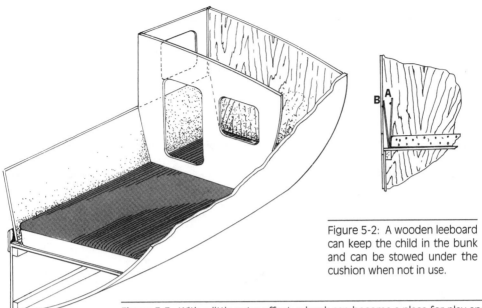

Figure 5-2: A wooden leeboard can keep the child in the bunk and can be stowed under the cushion when not in use.

Figure 5-3: With a little extra effort, a bunk can become a place for play and imagination. The panels shown can be made of plywood and dropped into the bunk using one or two catches to secure them. Make sure the holes are large enough so that children cannot get their heads stuck in them.

line holding the leecloth in such a way that a young child cannot undo it. A bowline is the most secure knot to use.

If the child is to sleep in the forepeak, the entire vee-berth can be made into a safe area for both sleeping and playing. First, increase the padding on the sides of the hull and make sure that there are no sharp corners to cause injury. Then, block off the vee-berth with a Dutch door or a drop-in plywood half-door, depending on the size of the forepeak. This will enable an adult to see into the forepeak but will keep your child in a contained area.

6: Supervision

Children should wear life jackets before even setting foot on the dock. Whenever children are playing on the dock, around the boat, or in a dinghy, an adult should be watching them. Life-threatening accidents can take only seconds to happen.

Insist that children not push or pull one another when on a dock or in a boat. Children are not as secure on their feet as adults and can easily fall. Don't let a young child steer the boat or operate an outboard motor unless carefully supervised. After all, you wouldn't let your three-year-old drive your car.

Always tell children what is about to happen. Warn them if you are going to tack, accelerate, or perform some other maneuver.

Treat the water with respect and do not take chances. You may get away with taking a chance once or twice, but eventually the odds will catch up with you.

Dropping Anchor

The anchor you use should give the best holding power for the type of seabed you will encounter. An anchor also should have adequate scope and weight, with a suitable line that is secured to the anchor on one end and to a strong point in the anchor locker on the other. But before you throw the hook over the side, consider: How long will you stay anchored? How near are other vessels or the shoreline? What are the direction and strength of the wind and tide? Are you staying on board while the anchor is set or are you leaving for a few hours or days? These questions should all be answered before you drop anchor. The following pages will help you determine the best method of anchoring in any situation.

7: The Name Game

Flukes, stocks, shanks, lightweight, kiting, CQR—parts and names of anchors can be confusing if you are a novice. In this section we'll try to clear the silt away from the various anchor parts and names. Figure 7-1 shows the types and parts of some of the most popular anchors.

Note the different types of anchor. Anchor A is a stockless CQR or plough anchor. Anchor B is a fisherman-type anchor used for rocky bottoms. Anchor C, a Danforth, is a stockless anchor, D is a Bruce anchor.

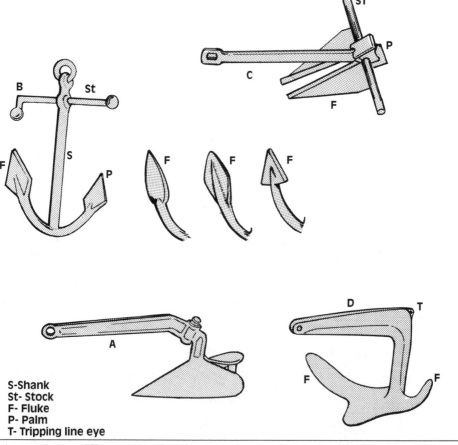

S-Shank
St- Stock
F- Fluke
P- Palm
T- Tripping line eye

Figure 7-1: Four different types of anchor. A is a stockless CQR or plough anchor. B is a fisherman or admiralty anchor with a conventional stock. C is a Danforth type stock-in-head anchor. D is the Bruce anchor. The labeled parts are as follows: S - Shank, St - Stock, F - Fluke, P - Palm, T - Tripping line eye.

The different parts of an anchor can also be confusing. The *stock* (ST in Figure 7-1) is used to turn the anchor so that the flukes will dig in. On early anchors, the stock was fixed at right angles to the arms, but on modern admiralty or fisherman anchors it slides through a ring in the *shank* (S) to make the anchor easier to handle. *Flukes* (F) can be any shape or size, and are sometimes called *palms* (P). The tip of the fluke is often referred to as the *bill*. Thus, when an anchor is cock-billed, it hangs ready to be lowered from the cathead. In other words, the bills are cocked at an angle to the deck, ready for lowering.

The rope holding the anchor is called the *line*, sometimes the *hawse* or *hawser*, the *cable*, or the anchor *rode* or *chain*. When chain is used for all or part of the anchor line it may have a stud across the middle of each link to make it run easier, in which case it is called *stud-link* chain. A *cable-laid* anchor line is made by twisting together three ordinary ropes, each of which is made from three ordinary strands. Anchor lines can be stowed in a *chain* or *cable* locker, access to which is down the *navel pipe*.

Anchors have different names depending on how and where they are carried. *Bower anchors* are usually a ship's largest anchors, carried in the bow of the boat with their cables permanently attached and running through hawse holes in the bow. A *breast anchor* is set off the side of the yacht. If the tidal current is pushing a docked yacht onto a seawall, the owner might set a breast anchor, as shown in Figure 7-2. Note how the lay of the yacht can be controlled by ad-

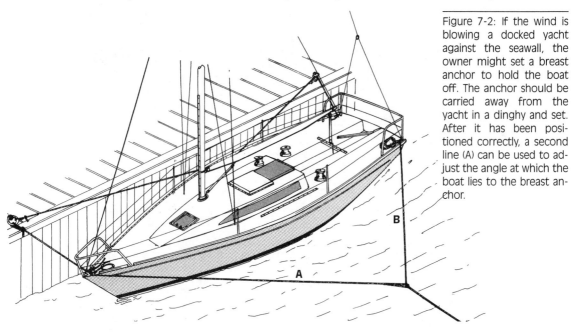

Figure 7-2: If the wind is blowing a docked yacht against the seawall, the owner might set a breast anchor to hold the boat off. The anchor should be carried away from the yacht in a dinghy and set. After it has been positioned correctly, a second line (A) can be used to adjust the angle at which the boat lies to the breast anchor.

justing the length of line A. A *drogue*, according to *The Oxford Companion to Ships and the Sea* by Peter Kemp (Oxford University Press, London and New York, 1976), should not be confused with a *sea anchor*. A drogue is dragged behind the vessel to prevent it from sailing too fast, while a sea anchor is used to hold the vessel's stern or bow to the wind in severe weather conditions. A spare anchor was originally known as the *kedge*, but today that name is often applied to almost any anchor not permanently attached to its anchor rode.

Another term once used around anchors is *becued*, an anchor line made fast to the crown of the anchor and seized with line to the shackle. If a becued anchor should foul or snag on something, the seizing will break and the anchor can be retrieved by hauling it aboard from the crown end. A more common way of retrieving a fouled anchor is with a *tripping line*, as shown in Figure 7-3. A tripping line is a thin (often ¼" or 6 mm) line attached to the tripping eye at the head of the anchor. If the anchor is fouled it can be pulled up with the tripping line. In practice, however, a tripping line can foul the anchor line, and can be tricky to pay out when setting the anchor. If there is no tripping line you might try running a *riding weight* down the cable in the hope that you can get it around the anchor shank and pull the hook free.

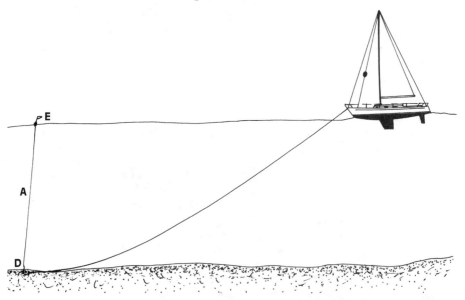

Figure 7-3: In areas where the bottom is known to be foul you might want to set a tripping line (A) on your anchor. The line is attached to the head of the anchor (D) and buoyed at point E. When the time comes to retrieve the hook, pulling on the tripping line will break it out easily.

An anchor can be lowered from the *hawse hole, bow roller, bow davit, cathead,* or even from the stern. The anchor is set by backing down on a reciprocal course causing the anchor to dig in. Then bearings should be taken on nearby stationary objects to ensure the boat is not dragging. Finally, an *anchor watch* should be set to make sure the anchor does not break. The anchor watchman will make sure a *black ball* is hoisted in the fore part of the boat to show other vessels that the boat is anchored. At night the watch will hoist an *all-around white light* in the forepart of the vessel, as shown in Figure 7-4.

When the time at anchor has ended, the anchor rode is *shortened* until the hook is *up and down.* It is then *tripped,* or *broken out.* The anchor is *aweigh* when it is hanging from the bow without touching bottom. This is also sometimes called *atrip.*

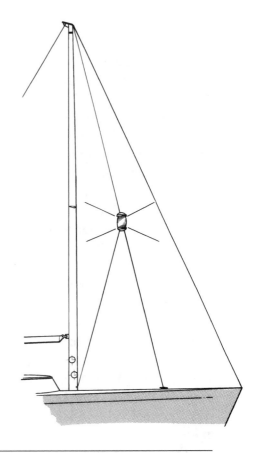

Figure 7-4: An anchor light (all-around white light) is set in the forepart of the boat at night.

Anchor usage has a complex terminology. While you don't have to know all the terms, it helps to know your navel pipe from your hawse hole.

8: Selecting an Anchor

Do you stand at the bow and just throw the hook over without giving much thought to the conditions in which you are anchoring? If so, you may find you are headed toward shoals. Anchoring properly and safely takes preparation. You should know the depth of water, the wind direction, the direction and strength of the tidal stream, the type of bottom, and the proximity of dangers. You should also know the draft of your boat, the anticipated length of your stay, and the rise and fall of tide. Each of these factors will affect the type of anchor you use and how much scope to pay out—and ultimately how safe your boat is.

The type of bottom, which can be easily read off any up-to-date chart, has a direct relationship to the type of anchor you should use. If you do not have a chart, an ordinary lead line can be armed (with a blob of tallow in the little recess in the bottom) and lowered to the seabed. Hauling it in again and inspecting the sediment stuck to the tallow will quickly show you what is down there.

The next job is to match the anchor to the bottom type to ensure holding power. A Danforth lightweight, for instance, holds well in a sand or mud bottom, as does a CQR, or plow, and a Bruce anchor. For rocky or coral bottoms, it is better to use a fisherman anchor (called an admiralty in Britain), or a grapnel anchor. Figure 8-1 shows a selection of anchor styles from various manufacturers. Many fisherman anchors are better known by other names. For instance, a fisherman with spear-shaped flukes is often known as a Nicholson, and one with triangular flukes as the yachtsman. The Luke anchor is a collapsible fisherman anchor that can be broken down into three pieces for easier stowage. The Herreshoff has wide diamond-shaped flukes for better holding power in shale or stony bottoms. Each of these anchors is basically the same style, but they have differences in the shape and size of their flukes, as shown in Figure 7-1.

Other types of anchor are the stockless, stock-in-head, lightweight, and kiting anchors. The best known stockless types are the CQR and the Bruce, neither of which needs a stock to orient itself properly. Stock-in-head types are those with the stock at the top of the anchor, like the Northhill or Danforth. The Danforth, Bruce, and CQR are also lightweight types, in that they do not rely on the weight of the hook to give them holding power, but on the ability of the hook to dig into the bottom and stay there even as the boat turns with the tide. Finally, the kiting anchor is an Australian variety that is supposed to kite to the required position if you cannot get your boat exactly where you want it. One wonders how the person doing the anchoring guides the anchor to the required spot.

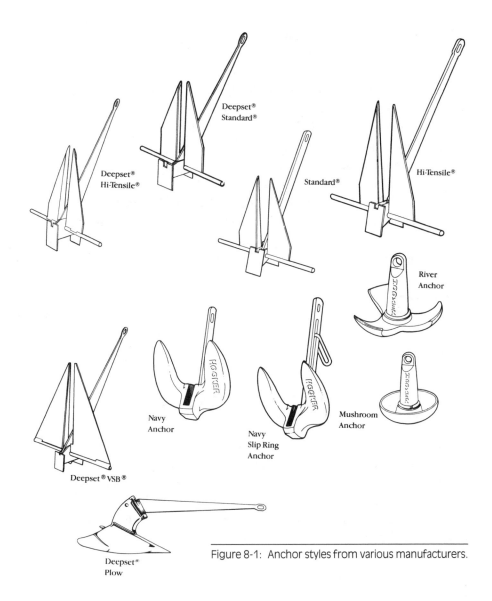

Deepset®
Standard®

Deepset®
Hi-Tensile®

Standard®

Hi-Tensile®

River
Anchor

Navy
Anchor

Navy
Slip Ring
Anchor

Mushroom
Anchor

Deepset® VSB®

Deepset®
Plow

Figure 8-1: Anchor styles from various manufacturers.

9: How Heavy Should Your Anchor Be?

This question has fascinated seafarers for hundreds of years. Today the picture is complicated by the lightweight, high-holding-power, and deep-penetration anchors that are available.

You can pick up advice on the weight of an anchor in any sailor's bar, but unfortunately that advice is usually limited to the owner's experience. For instance, someone might tell you he's used a Danforth 4s on his 28-footer for years without any trouble. He probably won't tell you he's never anchored overnight and has only dropped the hook for lunch in some secluded and well-protected cove. A Danforth 4s is suitable only for dinghies, such as Wayfarers, that are between 11 and 17 feet long.

The best anchor size recommendations are obtained either from the manufacturer or from a reputable authority such as Lloyd's Register of Shipping or the American Bureau of Shipping (ABS). Lloyd's gives a formula for the size of an anchor. From the formula, an equipment number is calculated, and from this equipment number the weight and size of the recommended anchor can be determined from tables. The equipment number also determines the size of the cable and how much chain may be used in conjunction with a synthetic rope cable.

Other anchor manufacturers also have tables that show what size anchor fits which boat. A table of anchors in current production in the U.S. is shown in Table 9-1.

10: How Much Chain Should You Use?

Many boat owners like to think they are more secure if they use an anchor line that is entirely chain, but both chain and rope have drawbacks and benefits. Chain is heavy, and needs to be stored somewhere, preferably as low in the boat as possible and in the middle of the hull. It also has limited shock-absorbing capacity, which means that in a heavy storm, when the line is fully taut, any shock loads from wave actions are transmitted directly to the boat. If your gear (anchor, anchor line, cleats, windlass, etc.) is oversized, all will probably go well, but a small weakness anywhere in the anchoring system might cause failure and the subsequent loss of your boat.

On the plus side, chain is virtually indestructible, and when anchoring in the tropics, where coral heads are likely to be present, chain is the anchor rode of choice. In fact, chain is the best choice if you anchor in areas with rocky bottoms. But remember, if you anchor in these areas you should use a fisherman anchor and be prepared to watch the line constantly. Anchoring in rocky bottoms can be an adventure because, as the tide changes and the anchor breaks

ANCHORS

Manufacturer	weight		Boat Length Max. LOA		Holding Power in hard sand lbs	Recommended Chain Length		Chain Diameter		Rode Diameter (minimum)		Comments
	Lbs	Kg	Feet	Meters		Feet	Meters	Inches	mm	Inches	mm	
Bruce												
Bruce BA10	4.4	2	15	4.6		15	4.6	3/16"	5	1/4"	6	
Bruce BA10	11	5	23	7		23	7.0	3/16"	5	3/8"	10	
Bruce BA 15	16.5	7.5	28	8.5		28	8.5	1/4"	6	3/8"	10	
Bruce BA20	22	10	32	9.6		32	9.8	5/16"	8	1/2"	13	
Bruce BA25	33	15	39	11.9		39	11.9	3/8"	10	5/8"	16	
Bruce BA30	44	20	46	14		46	14.0	3/8"	10	5/8"	16	
Bruce BA35	66	30	57	17.4		57	17.4	1/2"	12	3/4"	19	
Bruce BA40	110	50	72	22		110	33.5	5/8"	16	7/8"	22	
Bruce BA45	176	80	90	27.5	All Chain			3/4"	19	Use Chain Only		
Bruce BA50	242	110	106	32.3	All Chain			7/8"	22	Use Chain Only		
Bruce BA50	330	150	125	38	All Chain			1"	25	Use Chain Only		
Danforth												
S-160	3	1.4	10	3.0	800	3	0.9	3/16"	5	1/4"	6	
S-300	5	2.3	14	4.3	1600	3	0.9	3/16"	5	5/16"	8	
S-600	9	4.1	20	6.1	3200	3	0.9	3/16"	5	5/16"	8	
S-920	14	6.4	27	8.2	4900	4	1.2	1/4"	6	3/8"	10	
S-1300	16	7.3	32	9.8	6000	4	1.2	1/4"	6	3/8"	10	
S-1600	24	10.9	36	11.0	8000	5	1.5	5/16"	8	7/16"	11	
S-2000	42	19.1	41	12.5	10000	6	1.8	3/8"	10	1/2"	12	
S-3000	67	30.4	50	15.2	15000	8	2.4	1/2"	12	5/8"	16	
S-3500	105	47.6	57	17.4	19000	8	2.4	5/8"	16	3/4"	19	
H-500	5	2.3	19	5.8	2700	3	0.9	1/4"	6	5/16"	8	
H-960	12	5.4	27	8.2	6000	4	1.2	1/4"	6	3/8"	10	
H-1500	20	9.1	35	10.7	8750	5	1.5	5/16"	8	7/16"	11	
H-1800	35	15.9	38	11.6	11000	6	1.8	3/8"	10	1/2"	12	
H-3100	60	27.2	52	15.8	17000	8	2.4	1/2"	12	5/8"	16	
H-3600	90	40.8	58	17.7	20000	8	2.4	5/8"	16	3/4"	19	
H-4000	150	68.1	62	18.9	21000	8	2.4	5/8"	16	3/4"	19	
H-4400	190	86.2	65	19.8	23000	8	2.4	3/4"	19	1"	25	
D-375	3	1.4	15	4.6	2100	4	1.2	1/4"	6	3/8"	10	
D-750	8	3.6	25	7.6	4100	4	1.2	1/4"	6	3/8"	10	
D-1150	10	4.5	31	9.4	6500	5	1.5	5/16"	8	7/16"	11	
D-1650	15	6.8	37	11.3	8000	5	1.5	5/16"	8	7/16"	11	
D-2000	18	8.2	41	12.5	10400	6	1.8	3/8"	10	1/2"	12	
D-2500	31	14.1	44	13.4	14000	8	2.4	1/2"	12	5/8"	16	
D-3750	48	21.8	60	18.3	20000	8	2.4	1/2"	12	5/8"	16	
D-4400	65	29.5	65	19.8	24000	8	2.4	5/8"	16	3/4"	19	
T-570	3	1.4	19	5.8	3000	4	1.2	1/4"	6	3/8"	10	
T-1200	7	3.2	31	9.4	6000	4	1.2	1/4"	6	3/8"	10	
T-1800	9	4.1	38	11.6	9000	5	1.5	5/16"	8	7/16"	11	
T-2500	13	5.9	44	13.4	12000	5	1.5	5/16"	8	7/16"	11	
T-3000	17	7.7	50	15.2	15000	6	1.8	3/8"	10	1/2"	12	
T-4000	25	11.3	62	18.9	20000	8	2.4	1/2"	12	5/8"	16	
T-6000	41	18.6	72	21.9	28000	8	2.4	1/2"	12	5/8"	16	
T-7000	60	27.2	80	24.4	32000	8	2.4	5/8"	16	3/4"	19	
P-700	14	6.4	23	7.0	4250	4	1.2	1/4"	6	3/8"	10	
P-1000	18	8.2	27	8.2	4000	4	1.2	1/4"	6	3/8"	10	
P-1500	27	12.3	35	10.7	4000	5	1.5	5/16"	8	7/16"	11	
P-1800	33	15.0	38	11.6	4000	5	1.5	5/16"	8	7/16"	11	
VSB-900	7	3.2	27	8.2	1000	4	1.2	1/4"	6	3/8"	10	
VSB-1300	10	4.5	32	9.8	1400	5	1.5	5/16"	8	7/16"	11	
VSB-1900	13	5.9	41	12.5	2300	6	1.8	3/8"	10	1/2"	12	
VSB-2500	18	8.2	44	13.4	2900	6	1.8	3/8"	10	1/2"	12	
VSB-3600	25	11.3	59	18.0	3700	8	2.4	1/2"	12	5/8"	16	
Crosby												
Crosby CSS600	8.3	3.8	25	7.6	600	NR		NR		NR		
Crosby CSS1000	14.1	6.4	30	9.1	1000	NR		NR		NR		
Crosby CSS1500	24.3	11.0	38	11.6	1500	NR		NR		NR		
Crosby CSS2000	43	19.5	44	13.4	2000	NR		NR		NR		
Crosby CSS2500	52	23.6	50	15.2	2500	NR		NR		NR		
Crosby CSS4500	85	38.6	70	21.3	4500	NR		NR		NR		
Crosby CSS5000	95	43.1	90	27.4	5000	NR		NR		NR		
Hans C-Anchor												
2002	5.5	2.5	18	5.5	2500	NR		NR		NR		
2003	7.7	3.5	22	6.7	3500	NR		NR		NR		
2005	11	5.0	26	7.9	7500	NR		NR		NR		
2007	15.4	7.0	32	9.8	12500	NR		NR		NR		
2009	19.8	9.0	36	11.0	20000	NR		NR		NR		
2013	28.6	13.0	44	13.4	33000	NR		NR		NR		
2018	39.6	18.0	55	16.8	52000	NR		NR		NR		
2025	55	25.0	67	20.4	81000	NR		NR		NR		
2035	77	35.0	83	25.3	127000	NR		NR		NR		
2050	110	50.0	102	31.1	NA	NR		NR		NR		
Fortress												
FX-7	4	1.8	27	8.2	2800			3/16"	5	3/8"	10	
FX-11	7	3.2	32	9.8	3600			1/4"	6	3/8"	10	
FX-16	10	4.5	38	11.6	5000			5/16"	8	1/2"	12	
FX-23	15	6.8	45	13.7	8000			3/8"	10	5/8"	16	
FX-37	21	9.5	51	15.5	12000			3/8"	10	3/4"	19	
FX-55	32	14.5	58	17.7	16000			1/2"	12	7/8"	22	
FX-85	47	21.3	68	20.7	21000			1/2"	12	1"	25	
FX-125	69	31.3	80	24.4	27000			5/8"	16	1 1/4"	30	
Guardian												
G-5	3	1.4	16	4.9	1050			3/16"	5	1/4"	6	
G-7	4	1.8	22	6.7	1725			3/16"	5	3/8"	8	
G-11	6	2.7	27	8.2	2250			1/4"	6	3/8"	8	
G-16	7	3.2	33	10.1	3225			1/4"	6	3/8"	8	
G-23	13	5.9	41	12.5	4875			5/16"	8	1/2"	12	
G-37	18	8.2	47	14.3	7500			3/8"	10	5/8"	16	
G-55	29	13.2	53	16.2	10500			3/8"	10	7/8"	22	
G-85	42	19.1	62	18.9	13875			1/2"	12	1"	25	
G-125	65	29.5	72	21.9	18000			5/8"	16	1 1/4"	30	
SRS Anchor												

Model												
AC/SS	20	9.1			NS				NS	NS		
MF/SS	20	9.1			NS				NS	NS		
Flook Flying Anchor												
	6	2.7	13	4.0	NS				NS	1/4"	6	
	11	5.0	25	7.6	NS				NS	3/8"	8	
	22	10.0	45	13.7	NS				NS	1/2"	12	
Simpson Lawrence												
Harborfast SL0056915	15	6.8	25	7.6	NST	See Table 10-1						
Harborfast SL0056920	20	9.1	30	9.1	NST	See Table 10-1						
Harborfast SL0056925	25	11.3	37	11.3	NST	See Table 10-1						
Harborfast SL0056935	35	15.9	45	13.7	NST	See Table 10-1						
Harborfast SL0056945	45	20.4	55	16.8	NST	See Table 10-1						
Fisherman SL0056005	13.2	6.0			NST	See Table 10-1						
Fisherman SL0056006	17.6	8.0			NST	See Table 10-1						
Fisherman SL0056008	22	10.0			NST	See Table 10-1						
Fisherman SL0056009	26.4	12.0			NST	See Table 10-1						
Fisherman SL0056101	30.8	14.0			NST	See Table 10-1						
Fisherman SL0056102	39.6	18.0			NST	See Table 10-1						
Grapnel SL0056302	3.3	1.5			NST	See Table 10-1						
Grapnel SL0056003	5.5	2.5			NST	See Table 10-1						
Grapnel SL0056304	7	3.2			NST	See Table 10-1						
Grapnel SL0056305	13.2	6.0					NST	See Table 10-1				
Grapnel SL0056306	17.6	8.0					NST	See Table 10-1				
CQR SL0056303	15	6.8			26	7.9	NST	See Table 10-1				
CQR SL0056504	20	9.1			32.5	9.9	NST	See Table 10-1				
CQR SL0056505	25	11.3			32.5	9.9	NST	See Table 10-1				
CQR SL0056506	35	15.9			45.5	13.9	NST	See Table 10-1				
CQR SL0056507	45	20.4			58.5	17.8	NST	See Table 10-1				
CQR SL0056508	60	27.2			71.5	21.8	NST	See Table 10-1				
CQR SL0056509	75	34.0			71.5	21.8	NST	See Table 10-1				
Heavy duty CQRs												
CQR SL0056510	105	47.6					NST	See Table 10-1				
CQR SL0056511	140	63.5					NST	See Table 10-1				
CQR SL0056513	180	81.7					NST	See Table 10-1				
CQR SL0056515	240	108.9					NST	See Table 10-1				
CQR SL0056530	300	136.1					NST	See Table 10-1				
CQR SL0056540	400	181.5					NST	See Table 10-1				
CQR SL0056550	500	226.9					NST	See Table 10-1				
CQR SL0056560	600	272.2					NST	See Table 10-1				
Delta SL 0057404	9	4	22	6.8				1/4"	6			
Delta SL 0057406	14	6	30	9.1				1/4"	6			
Delta SL 0057410	22	10	39	11.9				5/16"	8			
Delta SL0057416	35	16	50	15.4				5/16"	8			
Delta SL 0057444	44	20	56	17				3/8"	10			
Delta SL 0057425	55	25	62	19.1				3/8"	10			
Delta SL 0057440	88	40	75	22.9				3/8"	10			
The Max (Adjustable)												
Max 15	24	10.9			30	9.1	NA	Recommend 10 ft chain	NS			Max Load = 1800 lbs
Max 17	38	17.24	45	13.7	450			Recommend 10 feet chain	NS	NS		Max Load = 2800 lbs
Max 20	52	23.6	60	18.3	1050			Recommend 10 feet chain	NS	NS		Max Load = 4500 lbs
Max 22	95	43.1	80	24.3	NA			Recommend 10 feet chain	NS	NS		Max Load = 6000 lbs
The Max (Rigid)												
Max 12	16	7.3					NA	Recommend 10 feet chain	NS	NS		Max Load = 1400 lbs
Max 15	20	9.1					NA	Recommend 10 feet chain	NS	NS		Max Load = 1800 lbs
Max 17	30	13.6	45	13.7			NA	Recommend 10 feet chain	NS	NS		Max Load = 2800 lbs
Max 20	40	18.2	60	18.3			NA	Recommend 10 feet chain	NS	NS		Max Load = 4500 lbs
Max 22	63	28.6	80	24.3			NA	Recommend 10 feet chain	NS	NS		Max Load = 6000 lbs
Paul E. Luke, Inc.												
No. 25	25		See Note B	Anchor chain and rode diameter will depend on boat size and weight and will be recommended at time of purchase								
No. 40	40		See Note B	Anchor chain and rode diameter will depend on boat size and weight and will be recommended at time of purchase								
No. 50	50		See Note B	Anchor chain and rode diameter will depend on boat size and weight and will be recommended at time of purchase								
No. 70	70		See Note B	Anchor chain and rode diameter will depend on boat size and weight and will be recommended at time of purchase								
No. 80	80		See Note B	Anchor chain and rode diameter will depend on boat size and weight and will be recommended at time of purchase								
No. 100	100		See Note B	Anchor chain and rode diameter will depend on boat size and weight and will be recommended at time of purchase								
No. 120	120		See Note B	Anchor chain and rode diameter will depend on boat size and weight and will be recommended at time of purchase								
No. 150	150		See Note B	Anchor chain and rode diameter will depend on boat size and weight and will be recommended at time of purchase								
No. 200	200		See Note B	Anchor chain and rode diameter will depend on boat size and weight and will be recommended at time of purchase								
No. 450	450		See Note B	Anchor chain and rode diameter will depend on boat size and weight and will be recommended at time of purchase								
No. 600	600		See Note B	Anchor chain and rode diameter will depend on boat size and weight and will be recommended at time of purchase								
No. 900	900		See Note B	Anchor chain and rode diameter will depend on boat size and weight and will be recommended at time of purchase								
American Yachting Series												
GPI-8	8	3.6	24	3.7	600	273						
GPI-13	13	6	33	10	900	409						
GPI-17	17	7.7	38	11.5	1200	545						
GPI-21	21	9.5	41	12.5	1500	682						
GPI-27	27	12.2	45	13.7	1800	818						
GPI-8GLV	8	3.6	24	3.7	600	273						
GPI-13GLV	13	6	33	10	900	409						
GPI-17GLV	17	7.7	38	11.5	1200	545						
GPI-21GLV	21	9.5	41	12.5	1500	682						
GPI-27GLV	27	12.2	45	13.7	1800	818						
Navy #910	10	4.5										
navy #915	15	6.8										
navy #920	20	9.1										
Navy #928	28	12.7										
Mushroom #508	8	3.6										
Mushroom # 510	10	4.5										
Mushroom #515	15	6.8										

NA = Not Available | NR = No Recommen | NST = Not Supplied See | NS = Not Supplied

Note that this gives an approximate idea of rope and chain S-L recommend

Note A: assume 2lbs of anchor for each foot of waterline length.

free, only to snag somewhere else, hold for a few minutes, and then break free again, your boat may be constantly on the move. Aboard the boat the dragging anchor usually brings loud noise and tremendous vibrations. Anchoring in these types of bottoms is to be avoided if possible.

When anchoring in a mud or sandy bottom, most yachtsmen usually use either a Danforth type anchor, a Bruce, or a CQR (plough) anchor. If you use these anchors exclusively, use nylon anchor rode; mud and sand bottoms have few obstacles to chafe the line. Nylon also has great shock-absorbing qualities, and is reasonably light compared to chain. It can be stored on a cable drum or flaked down on deck and lowered into the bilge. It doesn't rot or rust, and is easier to handle than chain.

There's a catch, however. When you drop the hook over the side and reverse the engine to set the hook, the pull on a nylon line is exerted almost directly from the yacht to the anchor as shown in Figure 10-1 (B). Unless you use a tremendous amount of scope, you may simply pull the hook out again. A better method is to install two or three fathoms (four to six yards or meters) of chain between the hook and the nylon line. This lowers the catenary of the line, as shown in Figure 10-1(A), and helps the anchor dig in better.

Unfortunately, you will either have to haul the fathoms of chain up by hand, or use a windlass that has both a drum (for the nylon line) and a chain gypsy to haul back the rode. If the rope is shackled to the chain, you will sometimes have a problem getting the shackle around the chain gypsy. To eliminate this problem, Simpson Lawrence makes special anchor lines with the rope spliced directly to the chain as shown in Table 10-1.

When using an anchor line, observe a few basic rules. First, make sure one end of the anchor line is tied to the anchor and the other to a strong point firmly bolted inside the anchor locker. I have seen sailors forget to tie the inboard end to the boat, with the result that the entire hook and line vanished beneath the waves. Second, make sure all shackles are moused. This means that a piece of wire is passed through the eye on the shackle pin and wound around the shackle to prevent the pin from unscrewing. Finally, make sure you have adequate anchor line for the depth of water you are in. Typically, the scope of the line should be three to five times the water depth.

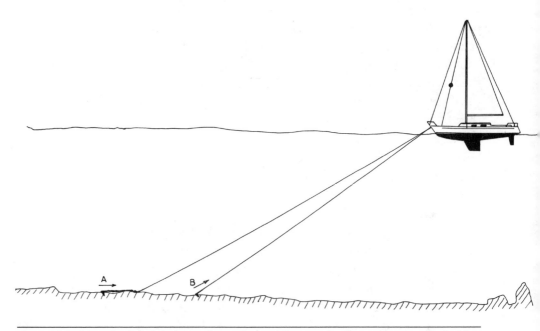

Figure 10-1: A length of chain between the anchor and the mooring line can increase the holding power of the hook. Note how at B with no chain the pull is directly toward the boat while at A the pull is tending along the seabed, allowing the anchor to dig in.

table 10-1

SIMPSON-LAWRENCE ANCHOR CHAIN AND ROPE GUIDE FOR SIMPSON-LAWRENCE WINDGLASS GYPSIES

Figure 2:	Simpson-Lawrence anchor chain and rope guide for Simpson Lawrence windlass gypsies						
Part #	Chain Type	Chain Size	Rope Size	Chain Length	Rope Length	Rode Length	
HM05G100	G7	1/4"	9/16"	5'	100'	105'	$113.95
HM10G150	G7	1/4"	9/16"	10'	150'	160'	$179.95
HM10H100	Hi Test	5/16"	9/16"	10'	100'	110'	$131.95
HM15H150	Hi Test	5/16"	9/16"	15'	150'	165'	$189.95
HM20H200	Hi Test	5/16"	9/16"	20'	200'	220'	$247.95
HM20H200C	Hi Test	5/16"	9/16"	20'	200'	220'	$266.95
HM10B100	BBB	5/16"	9/16"	10'	100'	110'	$129.95
HM15B150	BBB	5/16"	9/16"	15'	150'	165'	$189.95
HM20B200	BBB	5/16"	9/16"	20'	200'	220'	$244.95
HM20B200C	BBB	3/8"	5/8"	20'	200'	220'	$209.95
HM10S100	Super Link	3/8"	5/8"	10'	100'	110'	$169.95
HM15S150	Super Link	3/8"	5/8"	15'	150'	165'	$246.95
HM20S200	Super Link	3/8"	5/8"	20'	200'	220'	$326.95
HM25S250	Super Link	3/8"	5/8"	25'	250'	275'	$419.95
HM30S200C	Super Link	3/8"	5/8"	20'	200'	220'	$418.95
HM10BB100	BBB	3/8"	5/8"	10'	100'	110'	$171.95
HM15BB150	BBB	3/8"	5/8"	15'	150'	165'	$241.95
HM20BB200	BBB	3/8"	5/8"	20'	200'	220'	$323.95
HM25BB250	BBB	3/8"	5/8"	25'	250'	275'	$399.95
HM20BB200C	BBB	3/8"	5/8"	20'	200'	220'	$418.95
C denotes color coded anchor rode							
All ropes are New England Seaguard treated 3-strand Nylon rope and all anchor chain is hot dipped galvanized by Acco							

11: The Anchor Line

Does your boat sit at a mooring buoy all week while you are at work? While the boat is untended and subject to the vagaries of wind and tide, chafe may be working on your buoy line. Below the water, barnacles, slime, and other evil things may be working on your anchor line. Eventually, usually at the height of a storm, the combined effects of all these things could break the anchor line and drive your boat ashore, or worse yet, damage it enough to sink it.

To reduce chafe, look over the area near the bow chocks. Check that the fairlead or bow chock has no sharp edges. If it does, file or grind the edges smooth. Quite often the fairlead is set a little inboard and the line must run over the edge of the deck. While the edge might look like a smooth fiberglass corner, if it is reasonably acute, eventually it can cut your mooring line. To avoid this, cover the anchor rode with a piece of plastic tube, as shown in Figure 11-1. (A length of plastic garden hose is ideal.) About three feet is usually long enough. Make sure your mooring line can pass easily through the middle of it. Then make two small holes (about ⅛" diameter) at each end. Through these holes, pass about two feet of ⅛" line and secure it tightly. Now feed the tube onto the mooring line, making sure it covers the line where it passes over the potential trouble spots. Using a marlin spike, open the lay of the anchor or mooring rode and thread the ⅛" line through it. Do this at both ends of the plastic tube and secure it tightly so that it cannot move along the anchor rode. The tubing should be checked regularly to ensure that it is not abraded and cut by fixtures in the bow area. If it is, replace it.

Also check the stem. Is your stainless steel headstay fitting bolted along the front of the stem? If it is, can the anchor rode catch or chafe on the stainless steel or on the bolt heads?

If you lead the mooring line over a bow roller, check to see if the line can be chafed by the sides of the roller. Quite often, bow rollers are fabricated from

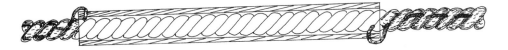

Figure 11-1: A length of plastic tubing reeved over the mooring line where it passes through a fairlead will reduce chafe on the anchor line.

welded stainless steel and the angles and edges are quite sharp. If the pull on your bow line is not square over the roller, chafe can easily occur.

Also check the bow cleats. They should be smooth and suitably sized to allow the anchor line to be wrapped around them. Often the anchor line is larger than can be fitted on the cleat, so you might have to make up a special cable with a spliced eye at the end. The eye is then fitted over the cleat and secured with a smaller line.

If you install your own mooring anchor, buoy, and line, make sure that the anchor is adequately sized for the boat. You can make a permanent mooring anchor from almost anything. A local boatyard uses huge poured concrete blocks about a yard (1 meter) on each side and about the same height. Another yard uses old railway carriage wheels. But you do not need to go to such extremes. A group of three good mushroom or plough anchors laid out 120 degrees apart, as shown in Figure 11-2, will provide many years of service after they have silted in (which takes about two years). The latest in permanent anchors are screw-in anchors, which have a screw thread on the bottom and penetrate up to six feet into the seabed. They are reputed to be able to hold up to ten times more than any other kind of permanent anchor.

When connecting anchor chains and lines, make sure that all the chains and shackles are made of the same material. If you use a brass shackle with an alu-

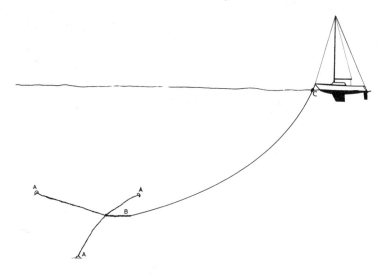

Figure 11-2: Three mushroom anchors will make a safe permanent mooring after they have silted in.

minum seizing wire, electrolytic corrosion could take place and render your chain useless. Remember also to mouse all shackles so that the pin cannot vibrate free. Figure 11-3 shows how to mouse an anchor shackle.

12: How Much Scope?

The depth of water and the draft of your boat govern where you can anchor, but the rise and fall of tide must also be taken into account. It would not do to anchor at half tide in twenty feet of water with forty feet of line out, when the tidal rise and fall is over thirty feet, as it is near Dinard, France, and in parts of the Bay of Fundy off the coast of Maine.

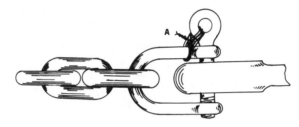

Figure 12-1: An anchor shackle should be properly moused to ensure that the shackle pin will not unscrew.

The wind and tidal streams (or currents) also affect where and how the boat will lie and how much scope to pay out. When anchoring, always motor upstream or upwind to drop the hook. If the wind and tide are opposing each other, choose the one that influences the boat most and go against it. Your boat is more likely to lay to a strong breeze than a weak tidal set.

The duration of your stay affects the size of hook and the amount of scope you use. For instance, you might use a smaller anchor and fairly short scope if you are stopping briefly in a secluded cove for lunch and a swim. A short stay might need only twice the water depth in scope. Leaving your boat unattended for a few days, on the other hand, may require laying out two anchors and anchor rodes up to seven times the depth of the water.

When paying out the anchor line, watch for dangers such as piers and other vessels. While you may be ideally situated when the tide is moving in one direction, when it changes you might get carried into shallow water, or against a pier or another boat. Before leaving your vessel for a long time, it is often worthwhile to stay onboard for a complete tidal circle to see where the change will take your yacht, and to adjust the scope as necessary.

This leads to another point: *don't* anchor close-by another boat; you could spend the evening worrying about a potential collision instead of having fun. You also will make the other skipper nervous. Some skippers will actually up-anchor and move away when another boat anchors nearby.

13: Selecting a Windlass

On boats up to about 28 feet, the anchor is usually so small that it can be handled by one person, and a windlass is not required. But on a yacht larger than thirty-five feet, the weight and size of an anchor make a windlass or a capstan essential if you don't want to hurt your back. The difference between a windlass and a capstan is that the barrel on a capstan is vertical, while on a windlass it is horizontal. In this section we'll use the term windlass and note any differences for a capstan.

The better windlasses have a barrel for rope and a chain gypsy to allow chain to be hauled in. The gypsy should be sized to fit the chain perfectly. A slipping chain can cause a serious accident. When sizing the barrel, make sure it is large enough so that you can wrap at least three turns of the anchor line around it. Any fewer turns and the line may slip.

If you intend to buy a manual windlass, it should be a double-action type— that is, the handle should pull the chain or line on both the pull and the push stroke. If you are buying an electric capstan or windlass, it should be sized to suit the anchor line, the anchor, *and* the ship's battery (or the battery size should be increased). Many electric windlasses will stall at 90 amps, that is, they will draw up to 90 amps of power before they stop. Look carefully at the maximum windlass rating. If it is very high, you should probably run the yacht's engine or generator when using it.

Next, look at where the windlass is to be mounted. Is the deck strong enough, or will it require reinforcement? Remember, too, that the bow roller should be strong enough to absorb shock loading as the bow rises in a seaway, and it should be firmly bolted in place. The introductory picture (13-1A) to

Figure 13-1A: A different method of stowing the anchor. In A both anchors are firmly lashed to prevent them moving in a seaway. In an emergency the lashings would have to be cut to set the anchor.

this section shows a typical bow roller unit. Note how the anchors are held securely in place by the pin passed through the tripping eye. Figure 13-1A shows a lash-up storage job. Neither of these anchors will be ready for use without cutting or untying the lashings. Another item, often neglected, is a strip of wood or metal between the bow roller and the windlass to stop the chain from scraping along the deck. It should be fitted so that it can be replaced should it become worn or damaged. Some boats also have a salt water washdown pump and wooden strips to guide muddy water from the chain and anchor back over the side before it dirties up the deck.

Figure 13-1B: The anchors are held with pins and can easily be set in an emergency provided the pins have not corroded.

14: Picking a Place to Anchor

Evening is falling and you are approaching your favorite anchorage. You pull around the headland expecting to drop the hook and have a quiet evening, but as you near your chosen spot you see that another boat is already there. Your first reaction is to look around for another mooring spot, but the cove is small and the best holding ground would put you near the other vessel. Moving closer inshore would put your boat into fairly shallow water, and anchoring farther out, near the channel, could put you very near the early morning ferry. The alternative is to head farther along the coast to another anchorage. Do you:

(a) Ask the other boat if you can moor alongside?
(b) Anchor near the other boat anyway?
(c) Anchor farther out, in a slightly more exposed position?
(d) Anchor near the channel and hope other vessels will see you?
(e) Find another mooring?

If your choice is (a) —and it should be only if you are good friends with the other boat's owner—lay out your own anchor and use your fenders and docklines to raft alongside the other boat so that both boats are swinging off both anchors. If you simply tie up alongside, or raft to the other vessel, the combined weight of both boats could exceed the holding power of the anchor and cause it to drag, putting both vessels in danger.

Choice (b) is foolhardy. If you anchor too close inside the other boat's swing circle, you may collide with it at the change of tide. Since the other vessel was anchored first, it is your duty to keep clear. In other words, should the yachts collide and damage result, your insurance company would have to pay.

Choice (c) is acceptable only if the weather forecast is suitable. If a front is forecast and the wind direction could change radically, you probably should not try an exposed anchorage. Neither should you try it if fog is forecast and other vessels may have to pass near the entrance to the cove.

Choice (d) is risky even under the best of conditions. A change of tide or wind direction could carry you into the channel, where you would be an obstruction to shipping.

Choice (e) is probably the safest course of action, but not always the most desirable, especially if you have sailed many hours to get to that particular cove.

Whatever choice you make, recognize the hazards when selecting an anchorage: the proximity of other vessels, a change in the tide or the weather, the nearness of shipping lanes, the depth of water, the nature of the holding ground, and the length of your stay. As a prudent seaman, consider these things carefully, not only for your own sake but also for the safety of others.

15: Is It Secure? Leaving a Boat in a Marina

How do you moor your boat in a slip or at dockside—with lines off the bow and stern and maybe a spring line? Or do you use fore and aft spring lines and breast lines? However you do it, it's important that the boat has enough slack to move around if the sea becomes choppy, or if another boat's wake creates waves.

Figure 15-1 shows a boat secured in a typical marina berth. Note how the lines are led at the bow and stern. If you have this type of berth, the boat is held well clear of any bulkheads or pilings, and there is no need for spring lines unless there is a strong tidal current. If two yachts are occupying a single slip, you and your neighbor may be able to secure both vessels away from the sides of the slips by putting a single breast line between them. If this is impossible you should tie up as shown in Figure 15-2, using bow and stern lines and fore and aft spring lines. This method will present a reasonably flat surface to the marina wall or dockside.

If severe weather is forecast, all dock lines should be doubled up—that is, the lines should be led to the dock and back to the boat. You should also check any places where chafe might occur to ensure that the lines do not abrade as the yacht moves around in the slip.

If the yacht is to be left against pilings, use a fender board to ensure that the piling cannot chafe against the side of the yacht. A fender board can easily be made from a piece of 2" × 10" (50mm × 250mm) wood 6 to 8 feet (2M to 3M) long, with holes drilled in the ends. When in use it is hung outside the fenders, against the piling, and ensures that the fenders cannot slip out from between the piling and the hull side.

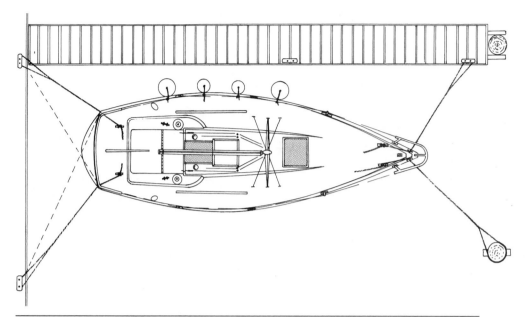

Figure 15-1: A yacht secured stern-to between pilings can be tied up from the bow and stern quarter. Some owners believe that the yacht's stern has less room to swing if the mooring lines are crossed, as shown by the dash lines. Note also that the fenders are placed at the widest part of the hull and that the larger fenders are placed on the outside of small-diameter fenders.

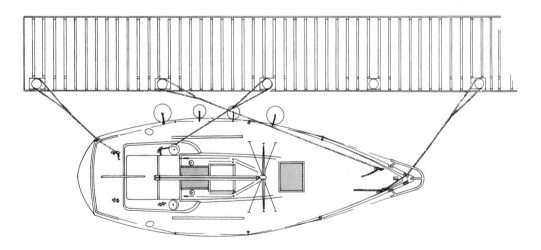

Figure 15-2: The most common method of securing a boat alongside a dock is using bow and stern breast lines and two springs. This boat is shown alongside a marina berth and is tied fairly snugly. Leave some slack in the lines if the boat is moored in an area of large tidal heights.

Dinghies

A short time ago, a client asked my company to design a new cruising yacht for him. After we talked and exchanged ideas, I realized this boat was to be designed around the size of the dinghy the client wanted to carry. In this case it was a large, rigid-bottomed inflatable that would be stowed on the cabin top. This in turn dictated the length of the cabin top, which ultimately determined the overall length of the boat. If the owner had been willing to compromise on the dinghy size, he could have had a smaller boat and saved a large amount of money. This situation is somewhat extreme, but it shows the importance that many people—especially those who cruise to remote areas—place on being able to carry and use a good dinghy.

In this section we'll look at how to choose the right dinghy for use as a yacht tender or for fun sailing, where to stow it, how to tow it, and how to get it ready for a cruise.

16: Selecting a Dinghy

How do you choose the right dinghy? Is it the one that has the attractive varnished gunwale, or the one with three seats and room for eight people, or even the one that can be dismantled into two or three sections? While these are some of the features you might want to consider for your dinghy, they are not the most important ones.

When choosing a dinghy, consider its features. First, can it be stowed on board? Some people like to stow the dinghy on the foredeck, and on some yachts that's the only place to put a hard-bottomed craft. Others like to carry the dinghy on the cabin top or tow it behind the boat. If the boat is large enough (usually 30 to 35 foot LOA is the minimum), the cabin top may be a good option. If you plan to tow the dinghy, give some thought to what you will do in heavy weather: a towed dinghy may fill with water in rough seas and may be lost or sunk.

If you do not have room to stow a dinghy on deck, you might want to select an inflatable. Even a large inflatable can be stored in a cockpit locker and blown up when required. For instance, the 9-foot Avon Rover is ideal as a yacht tender. It has wooden bottom planks, will carry up to four people easily, and weighs about 70 pounds. It takes only a few minutes to inflate and can be towed or hoisted aboard with little effort. I use mine with a six horsepower outboard that gets it onto a plane with one person aboard. When collapsed and stowed, it takes up a space about 42" × 24" × 14" (107 × 62 × 36 cm).

A second feature to consider when selecting a dinghy is whether it has adequate flotation to support the number of people you intend to carry plus their gear. Third, take a look at the stability of the dinghy. If it tips over too easily, you may not want to carry small children or pets in it. Size is another important factor: if you normally sail with a crew of six and the dinghy only holds two people, it will require a number of trips to get the crew aboard. You should also choose a dinghy that has some form of protection around the gunwale. A rubber chafing strip is the best way to avoid damaging the yacht's topsides when you come alongside.

A last and often disregarded factor is the weight of the dinghy. Dinghies get dragged over beaches, carried portage style along docks and piers, and must be launched and retrieved. A heavy dinghy will be used less and less because of the effort required to launch it unless you can afford a trailer specifically for the dinghy, but this creates the problem of storing the trailer while the dinghy is in use.

17: Fitting Out a Dinghy

A prudent seaman is always prepared, or so says the old adage. Even the dinghy should be prepared against unforeseen events. Many sailors who power their dinghy with an outboard often forget to put oars aboard. Ideally, oars should be secured with a short lanyard so that, if the dinghy capsizes, the oars cannot float away.

Remember also that oars require oarlocks. (Many sailors, particularly the French, use one oar over the transom and scull with it, but this requires an oarlock in the transom or a notch cut out of the transom.) The oarlocks should have a line passed through the oarlock hole and secured to a strake or with a stopper knot. Oarlocks should be removed when coming alongside a yacht to ensure that they do not damage the topsides when the dinghy bumps the yacht.

Quite often, the act of launching a dinghy off a yacht scoops several gallons of water, making a bailer another essential. The bailer, too, should be secured by a light lanyard fastened to a sole board or strake (or in the case of an inflatable, to one of the handles). Additionally, a large sponge is a useful item that can be stowed in the bailer.

Make sure the dinghy has a long painter (a length of line used to moor the dinghy to a boat or dock) securely fastened to a bow ring. Ideally, this ring should be situated low on the stem to lift the bow slightly when the boat is being towed.

If you are going to use an outboard, make sure the transom is strong enough to carry it. Also size the engine to suit the dinghy. Many dinghies are not intended for high speeds, and overpowering them by using a larger engine can result in serious accidents.

If you will be crossing a harbor at night in your dinghy, you should have either navigation lights or a flashlight on board. The international COLREGS (*International Regulations for the Prevention of Collisions at Sea*) state that a dinghy under 12 feet long should have at least one white all-around light. Again, this should be tied securely in place.

Make sure the dinghy has a drain bung that can be removed to empty it once you have the dinghy on board or ashore.

Larger dinghies may also carry a small anchor. It need not be much more than a lunch hook (a light anchor dropped for an hour or two while the crew has lunch), but a small hook and several fathoms of nylon rode will give the owner a much greater sense of security. If the engine fails or you want to go fishing you may decide to anchor.

18: Stowing a Dinghy

Not every sailor likes to use an inflatable and many prefer a hard-bottomed dinghy, which may pose a problem when trying to stow it.

Many small boats tow the dinghy behind the yacht, and when it really needs to be stowed they put it on the cabin top, in spite of the reduced visibility this creates for the helmsman. Another option is to use a dinghy that divides into two to three pieces. There are several on the market.

On larger boats, the dinghy is often stowed in davits mounted on the transom. As long as the dinghy is no wider than the beam of the boat this method is perfectly acceptable. The dinghy should have a cover, however, and should not become the receptacle for all the gear that has no other place to go: ideally, the dinghy's fenders and mooring lines should be the only items stowed there. A dinghy filled with heavy gear can weigh down the boat's stern and seriously degrade performance, or even break the davits off the boat. Figures 18-1, 1A

Figure 18-1

Figure 18-1A and B: On this boat, designed by the author, the radar arch has fold-down dinghy davits, on which the dinghy is stowed. 18-1A shows how the arch looked when the davits were folded away, while B shows them folded down holding a dinghy.

and B show a radar arch with davits as designed for a cruising boat by the author.

Other stowage positions are on the afterdeck, or middeck. Chocks may be wood alloy or molded into a fiberglass hull to make a place for the dinghy. Figure 18-3 shows some variations.

The dinghy can be stowed right side up, in which case it can be used to stow fenders, lines and awnings, or it can be stowed upside down, in which case it will provide protection for open hatches in rainy weather. When the dinghy is fitted on the cabin top, some method of launching is required. The easiest method is to use the main boom with the main halyard taken to the end of the boom. If the boat is a ketch, the mizzen boom can be used.

On older, very large vessels the dinghy often has its own davits somewhere along the side of the yacht into which it can be hoisted after use. Some yachts have a davit on the foredeck that serves both the dinghy and the anchor.

Note that no matter where you stow the dinghy, it should be tightly secured when not in use. The most common method is with webbing straps taken across the dinghy hull. If the dinghy is mounted in transom davits, it is more difficult to secure, but lashing it tightly against the davits is usually an acceptable method.

When the dinghy is in the water you don't need to haul it out every night if you have some

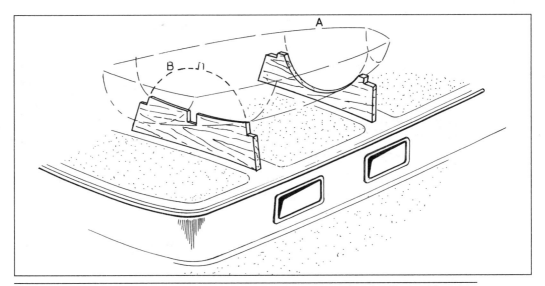

Figure 18-2: The wooden chocks shown here are suitable for mounting the dinghy either right side up or upside down.

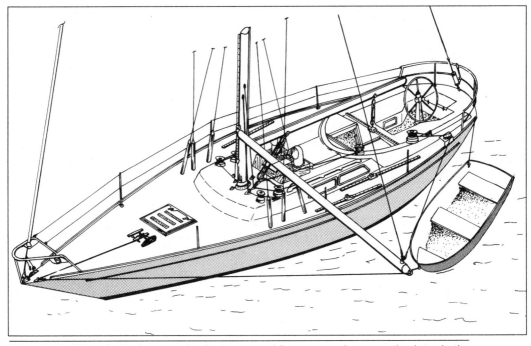

Figure 18-3: If the dinghy bangs under the transom while on a mooring, an option is to rig the spinnaker or winging-out pole and moor the dinghy fore and aft alongside.

method of securing it to prevent it from banging against your boat. Some larger vessels carry a boat boom that is extended at 90 degrees to the centerline of the yacht, and the dinghy or dinghies are streamed from it. Smaller yachts can use a variation of this technique and set the spinnaker pole athwartships. The dinghy can then be secured to the pole end and to the transom, as shown in Figure 18-3.

Of course, if there is a tidal set, the dinghy can be streamed astern. Quite often, however, when the tide changes, the dinghy will fetch up under the transom or bang alongside the hull. While trailing it astern is a good short term solution, a fore-and-aft moor is an even better one.

19: Towing a Dinghy

Few sailors give much thought to how their dinghy should be towed, but the drag on the yacht can increase dramatically if the dinghy is towed incorrectly. Incorrect towing also can result in a swamped or sunk dinghy.

First, check the dinghy's painter and make sure it is not abraded, that the splice is secure, and that it is of adequate length. Next, check the towing eye. Make sure it is not corroded and that the bolts securing the eye will not pull out under load.

When leaving the dock, keep the dinghy on a short tether. It should be just loose enough to allow you to back down, if needed, without jamming the dinghy under the transom. As soon as you are underway and up to your normal cruising speed, look to see where the crests of the stern waves are and then ease the dinghy out until it is sitting just forward of the crest of the second or third wave. In this position, the dinghy is almost surfing on the stern waves. If it is allowed to drop behind the crest, the yacht will be pulling it up the wave face. This imposes additional strain on the towing line. If the dinghy is too far in front of the wave crest it may surge down the wave and proceed in a series of surges and jarring snaps as the towline slackens and then takes up again. This will soon break the towline and/or the dinghy. If you are really unlucky, the dinghy could even surge off to one side and capsize when the towline snaps taut again.

20: Inflatables

Inflatables are rapidly becoming the tender of choice among experienced sailors. They can be stowed in a locker when not in use. They can be inflated with a simple hand or foot pump. They are light enough to be launched by one or two people, and they are safe. They also will not damage the topsides if you collide with your yacht after dinner and drinks.

If you intend to buy an inflatable for use as a small vessel used to carry people to a larger boat or yacht, keep these points in mind. First, a wooden-bottomed boat is much easier to board. Second, if you intend to use an outboard, a dinghy with a wooden transom is the best bet, because the outboard can be easily mounted or unmounted on it. Make sure the transom has a bung hole so that you can drain water out easily. A third feature to look for is multiple inflation tubes. While they are slightly more cumbersome to blow up, multiple tubes give you the chance of making it to shore or to your boat should the dinghy be inadvertently holed.

Fourth, look for well-secured towing points, handles, and a lifeline around the sides. The lifeline will help should you have to pull someone out of the water. Molded-in oarlocks are the fifth most important feature. If the outboard fails, you can row ashore or back to your boat.

If necessary, an inflatable can be towed astern, although it tends to veer and steer quite capriciously under tow. It also can be hoisted into davits and lashed in place.

21: The Sailing Dinghy

Have you ever watched a sprightly little dinghy sail across the harbor, envying the sailor at her helm, or admired the two men aboard a Flying Dutchman on a screaming reach? If you have, then maybe there's a sailing dinghy in your future. A sailing dinghy can be tremendous fun, whether it is an Olympic class 470 or a little Optimist with two excited children on board.

First, you should decide what boat you'd like, whether you want to race or cruise, or whether you simply want to get out on the water and have fun.

Cruising in a dinghy is usually done by one or two people in a boat only large enough to hold them and their camping gear. You sail in daylight from one camping ground or comfortable beach to the next.

Racing, on the other hand, demands effort both on the race course and ashore. Getting the boat ready requires considerable effort, and racing requires mental as well as physical skills. Ask the local yacht club what type of dinghies they use. Most clubs have a dinghy fleet, even if it is only for frostbiting (sailing in winter).

If you want to go ahead and get a dinghy, consult a local expert about the cost and maintenance. Also ask about a place to keep the boat. Often, a dinghy can be either stored at the yacht club, carried on top of a car, or carried on a trailer and stored at home.

If you do not sail, then enroll at the nearest sailing school that gives classes for the type of boat you want to buy. If that option is not available, try to find a friendly sailor and get him to teach you. If you intend to race, make sure you learn how to rig, tune, and balance the boat out for best speed. After you've learned the ins and outs, enter a fun race or two, to get a feel for your skill level. It doesn't matter if you place dead last. If you noticed how the others sail and if you've learned something, the outing was worthwhile. Ask other sailors how they tune their boats, how they sail them, and gradually you'll find your skills will improve and your position in the fleet will rise.

Sails and Sail Control

K nowing how to adjust your sails properly is critical for several reasons. First, when a sail flaps it is damaging to the fabric and structure so the less you let it flap the longer it will last. Second, well adjusted sails permit you to sail faster and more comfortably, with less heel and a smoother motion. Third, properly set sails require less time and effort to adjust and keep trimmed.

In this section we'll look at trimming individual sails, and then setting them to act in concert. We'll also look at spinnakers, both the racing and cruising kind, and at how to use less well known sails, such as staysails and mizzens, more effectively.

How do you trim your mainsail? Do you put it up and forget it, or do you adjust it for every puff? If you sail regularly, you should know what the mainsail controls can do for you.

The halyard holds up the sail but it also controls the luff of the sail and, to some extent, the shape. First, hoist the sail and sheet it in. Check the luff. If you see horizontal creases, tighten the halyard; if vertical creases show, ease the halyard. Do the same along the foot, easing or tightening the outhaul if horizontal or vertical creases are present. Figure 22-1 shows where to look.

With the headsail set and drawing, and the boat sailing as near to close hauled as possible, adjust the sheet and traveler until the boom is on or a few degrees below the yacht's centerline, and the leech of the sail has a fairly taut look to it. Look up from under the boom at the battens. The outer end of the bottom batten should be a few degrees higher than the boom, the middle two battens should be a few degrees lower than the boom, and the top batten should be either parallel to the boom or a few degrees high of it. If the battens are not set correctly, watch the telltales and battens, tighten the sheet and watch the telltales on the leech. They should stream aft without lifting or curling behind the sail. If the top ones curl, ease the sheet slightly. Afterward check the battens once again. You'll usually find that they are now set just right.

After adjusting the boom, check the entire sail. If the outhaul has been set properly the luff may have a slight bubble and there will not be any creases either horizontally or vertically.

The traveler should be adjusted in conjunction with the sheet. It should be thought of as similar to a flap on an airplane, in that it sets the sail at the correct angle of incidence. Most boats require that the main boom be either on the centerline or slightly to leeward of it when the boat is sailing to windward. Use the traveler to put the boom where you want it. When the wind gusts up and the helmsman has to use a lot of rudder to keep the boat on course, use the traveler to ease the mainsail down to leeward. This way the sail shape will not need adjustment when you haul it back in again. When you round a mark or come from a beat to a reach, the main should be eased *on the traveler first*. This will retain the sail shape while altering its angle of incidence to the wind.

At this stage the mainsail is set. If you are a racer, however, there is much more to do to get the last ounce of power out of it. The sail will need to be adjusted to compensate for fluctuations in the wind's strength.

If the wind lightens, you will need to ease the outhaul and halyard to make the sail deeper. You will probably have to move the traveler further to windward and ease the mainsheet to open the mainsail leech and let the air flow freely out of the sail. In very light winds, move the crew to leeward to help the sail maintain a better shape.

As the wind increases, the sail gets fuller and the draft moves aft. To remove fullness in the lower third of the mainsail, tighten the outhaul. To remove fullness aloft, tighten the baby stay to pull the middle of the mast forward. The Cunningham eye is used to pull the draft forward—that is, to move the deepest part of the sail's belly forward. It should be used sparingly and the draft should be watched carefully as the Cunningham is tensioned.

When the Cunningham is at its limit, it is time to use a flattening reef. The flattening reef, as its name implies, is pulled down to flatten the lower third of the sail. Taking it in makes the sail flatter without losing

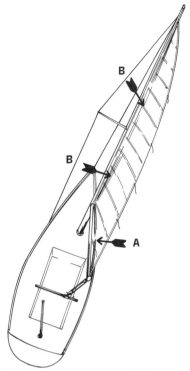

Figure 22-1: A shows where foot creases will occur if too much outhaul is used. B shows where vertical creases may occur if the halyard is overtensioned.

actual sail area. A flatter mainsail has the effect of allowing the boat to stand up straighter and sail faster as the breeze strengthens. Note that if your boat does not have a flattening reef, taking up on the halyard and tightening the outhaul produces a similar effect.

To make the middle and upper part of the mainsail flatter you should use mast bend. Tension the baby or midstay to pull the middle of the mast forward and make the top two thirds of the mainsail flatter.

How often do you sail along with the leech of your headsail flapping like a pigeon headed for food? Not often, you say, but do you know how to get the best shape out of your headsail?

First, hoist it and tighten the halyard so that when the sail is sheeted in there are no creases in the luff of the sail. Horizontal creases mean the luff is too slack and the halyard should be tightened. Creases parallel to the headstay mean that the halyard is too tight, so ease it.

Next, look at the sheeting position. As a first step, the line of the sheet from the block to the corner of the sail should bisect the angle of the clew, as shown in Figure 23-1. Remember, though, that the sail is longer on the leech than on the luff, so the angle bisected is not quite equal on both sides. To allow for the longer leech, move the sheet lead car forward one or two holes. Now look at the telltales. (You should have at least three, spaced equidistant up the luff of the sail, each about eight inches long and about nine inches back from the headstay, as shown in Figure 23-2.) If the top tell-tale lifts when you are hard on the wind, the lead is too far aft. Move it forward one hole and try again. Keep trying until all the telltales lift together.

These are the basic rules for setting the headsail. In lighter winds there should be slightly more foot round in the genoa. Therefore, the lead should be slightly farther forward, and as the wind increases the lead should be pulled aft to flatten the sail. Remember, too, that the halyard should be tightened as the wind increases, and this will usually require a change in the sheet tension. If the halyard tension is maxed out, use a Cunningham eye to pull the luff down and move the draft forward again.

When adjusting the sail, note its overall shape and the proximity of the leech to the spreaders. Any change in the tension of the halyard or sheet will change the position of the sail relative to the spreaders. It often helps to put two or three wraps of tape on the spreader-ends at 3" and 6" intervals to enable you to gauge how far the sail is from the spreader.

Next, look at the leech of the sail. Is it flapping? If it is, take up on the leech line, but only until the flapping stops. If this produces a large hook in the leech, the sail should probably be recut. If the bottom of the sail flaps, the foot line should be adjusted. On some boats the foot of the genoa is cut so full that it will flap no matter what you do. In this case a piece of shock cord with a small

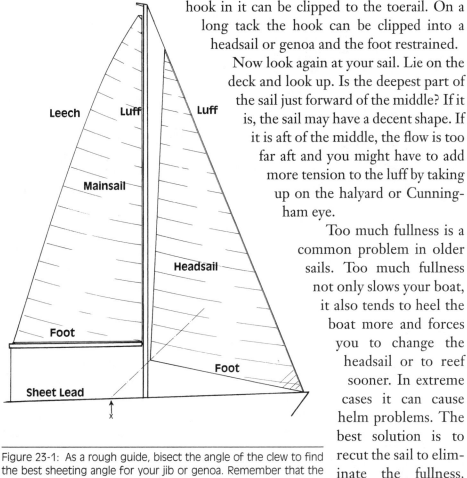

hook in it can be clipped to the toerail. On a long tack the hook can be clipped into a headsail or genoa and the foot restrained.

Now look again at your sail. Lie on the deck and look up. Is the deepest part of the sail just forward of the middle? If it is, the sail may have a decent shape. If it is aft of the middle, the flow is too far aft and you might have to add more tension to the luff by taking up on the halyard or Cunningham eye.

Too much fullness is a common problem in older sails. Too much fullness not only slows your boat, it also tends to heel the boat more and forces you to change the headsail or to reef sooner. In extreme cases it can cause helm problems. The best solution is to recut the sail to eliminate the fullness. That is a temporary solution, however,

Figure 23-1: As a rough guide, bisect the angle of the clew to find the best sheeting angle for your jib or genoa. Remember that the leech is longer than the luff and move the sheet block forward one or two holes until all the telltales are flying properly.

which will last only about one more season at best. Old sailcloth distorts easily after it has been recut. If you decide not to get the sail recut, taking up on the halyard, Cunningham, and sheet will eliminate some fullness, but the sail will not be as fast as a new one.

Next we come to the use of headstay tension. A tight headstay will help you go to windward faster. It, too, can help eliminate fullness in the sail. But headstay tension is something to be used carefully. For instance, in flat water a tight halyard and less-than-tight headstay are better. The sail is not so powerful, but the overall effect is to flatten the entry and help pointing.

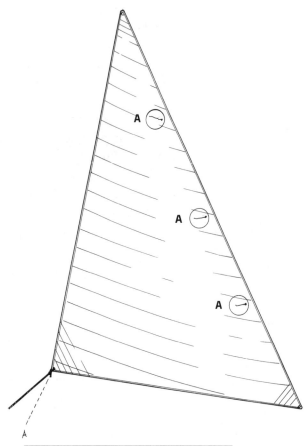

Figure 23-2: You should have telltales (A) along the luff of the genoa for best performance.

In a seaway, the opposite is better. A tight headstay and a slack halyard will give you more luff roundness, which translates into more power and less pointing ability, but helps the boat drive through the waves better. If you cannot adjust the headstay on your boat, it is best to set it up as tightly as possible, assuming that it will be less than ideal in heavy winds, but tighter than usual in lighter winds.

While the above rules can be applied to most boats, they may not be ideal for all. If you have any doubts about the effectiveness of your headsail, you should experiment to see what you might do to get extra speed.

24: Preparing a Spinnaker

While it appears to be a mundane chore, getting a spinnaker ready is an important part of using it. If the sail is not packed correctly, it can twist as it is hoisted and wrap around the headstay. Even worse, the man on the foredeck might mistakenly connect the halyard to the clew and cause the sail to be hoisted upside-down. A properly packed spinnaker can help the racing crew make a perfect set and gain several boat lengths.

When we were racing we used to pack the spinnaker immediately after it was taken down. During one overnight race, the *"all hands"* call was heard and we scrambled to get the sail in. As soon as it was below we repacked it, cleaned up, and turned in. The only person who didn't turn in was the cook, who had lost his pajamas in the scramble. The loss was not solved until the next day's race, when, at the Royal Yacht Squadron line off Cowes, we set the spinnaker. The brightly colored pajamas floated out of the sail and were borne away on the morning breeze amid guffaws from the other crews around us.

Lighter spinnakers (usually less than ¾-ounce) should be flaked into their containers, be it a turtle, sausage, or spinnaker bag. To flake the sail, first find the head. Hook the shackle or swivel over a coat hook or similar object. Work down

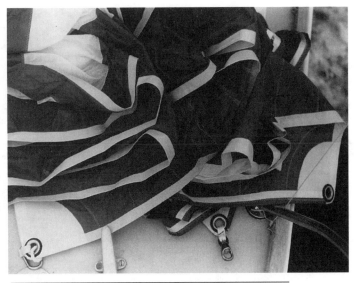

Figure 24-1: A flaked spinnaker ready to be packed with all three corners and the luff tapes visible.

Figure 24-2: A fully packed sail with the corners easily visible. Note that the clews and head are clearly marked.

Figure 24-3: A spinnaker stopping bucket can be made by cutting the bottom out of a sturdy plastic bucket, and gluing a strip of wood down one side of it to help you remove the elastic bands easily.

Figure 24-4: A spinnaker shown here between two masts, for a larger boat should be stopped with legs to enable it to be preset. It is easy to break this sail out by pulling the sheet and pole aft after the sail has been hoisted and cleated off.

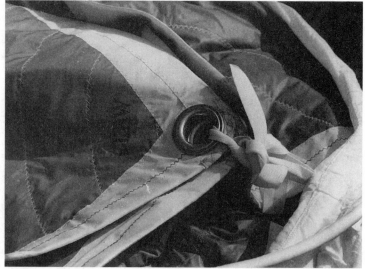

Figure 24-5: The end of the packing job: A nicely stowed spinnaker with the corners tied off.

each side in turn, gathering both luffs into pleats. Hold the luffs and clews and work across the bottom. When you have finished you'll have an armful of pleated spinnaker, as shown in Figure 24-1. Have another crewman stuff the belly of the sail into the turtle while you hold the pleated edges out. The last parts of the sail to go into the turtle are the edges, followed by the head and clews. These should be laid on top of the stuffed sail as shown in Figure 24-2, or tied off inside the bag.

Heavier spinnakers should be stopped. Stops prevent the sail from opening until it is hoisted and the halyards cleated off. If you don't already have one, you'll need to make or buy a spinnaker stopping bucket. Take a strong plastic bucket, discard the handle, cut the bottom out of it, and glue a wooden strip down one side (this makes it easier to get the elastic bands off it, as shown in Figure 24-3). Place large (about $\frac{1}{16}$" × 3" or 1 mm × 75 mm) elastic bands around the bucket, in sufficient numbers to accommodate the height of the spinnaker. Now pass the head of the sail through the top of the bucket and flick an elastic band off every 18" (about .5M) as you pass the sail through. Remember to run down each leech and hold them together as the sail is fed through the bucket. Also gather the belly of the sail and roll it tightly so that the sail is tightly held by the bands. If the sail is for a small boat (under 30 feet), it can be stopped all the way until the clews pass through the bucket. Note that elastic bands make it easier to stop the sail, but you can also use wool and tie stops every three feet or so. You should tie a wool stop only once around the sail or the stop may not break.

If you are sailing short-handed or on a large vessel, you might want to stop the spinnaker with "legs" to enable you to preset the pole and guy before hoisting. Starting at the top, stop the sail in the conventional manner and work downwards. When you have passed the midpoint of the sail, stop and remove the bucket. Now start at each clew and work inwards until you reach the middle. This gives the stopped sail "legs," as shown in Figure 24-4.

The last step is to stuff the sail into its bag. Feed the middle in first and follow with the head and both clews so that they end up on the top of the pile. Tie off the corners, as shown in Figure 24-5, and the job is done.

25: Setting a Spinnaker

The wind has changed and it's time to set the spinnaker, but there are only two of you on deck and you're not sure if you can handle it. However, with careful preparation, hoisting the spinnaker can be reduced to a series of simple steps.

While one person is sailing the boat, the other can get the spinnaker ready. Leave the genoa and mainsail up and drawing to keep the boat moving.

Carry the turtle forward and clip it onto the leeward rail a few feet aft of the bow, or hook the turtle into the bow pulpit if you normally do that. At this stage do not open the turtle, as seas breaking over the lee bow might pull the spinnaker out.

Now make sure the pole topping lift and spinnaker foreguy are uncleated. Set the inboard end of the pole in the mast cup or pin, hook up the topping lift and foreguy, and feed the afterguy through the outboard end of the pole. Hook the afterguy into the spinnaker clew while the sail is still in its turtle. Follow that by hooking the sheet to a stanchion next to the turtle. Close the turtle again with the shackle of the guy inside.

Bring a halyard forward. Ideally, it should be the leeward spinnaker halyard, which, if it has been stowed at the mast, will need to be carried forward around the headstay and then passed behind the genoa, before being hooked into the head of the spinnaker inside the turtle.

Now preset the pole—that is, raise it until it is horizontal and pull it aft slightly. As soon as the sail is set, the guy will be pulled aft to the correct position. Make sure you do not pull the guy out of the turtle while you are presetting the pole.

A quick recap: The guy is hooked on, the halyard is hooked on, the pole is up with the foreguy and topping lift tight. The sheet can now be hooked into the sail. The reason you did not do this before is that the sheet lies along the leeward side of the boat and is often tugged by the force of the water, which might pull the spinnaker into the water.

Now for the actual set. It is easier if the spinnaker has been carefully stopped, but even if it hasn't, here's how to do it. First, take up on the halyard as fast as possible. The easiest way for one person to do this is to make sure the halyard runs through a rope clutch and the clutch is closed. Then put one turn on a winch and haul away. (Use one turn on the winch until the halyard is 95 percent of the way up. Only when the halyard becomes too heavy to haul hand-over-hand should you put more turns on the winch and use a handle. Too many turns when first hauling the halyard up will cause an override. Having at least one turn on the winch ensures that, should the spinnaker fill half way up, you will have time to get more turns before the full force comes on the halyard.) A second person should pull the guy aft until the spinnaker is at the end of the pole and then cleat off the guy. Now the sail is secure at the guy and head, and the sheet is flogging. (Don't let the sail flog too long or the snap shackle could flip undone and come off the clew.) Take up on the sheet (if the sail is stopped this will break out the stops), and the sail is now drawing. Now drop the genoa, clean up the deck, and sail the boat.

26: Spinnaker Trim

How do you trim the spinnaker? If you hoist it and forget it, you could be heading for a wrap—a spinnaker wrap, that is, around the headstay. To get the very best out of your spinnaker requires constant vigilance and care.

There are three golden rules to trimming a spinnaker. First, the pole should be set perpendicular to the direction of the wind, as shown in Figure 26-1, to project the maximum area of spinnaker to the wind. If the helmsman is steering a steady course and the wind is reasonably steady, this is easy, but when the helmsman wanders and the wind is gusty, it can be quite a job.

Second, the clews should be level. Only in very light winds should the pole end be slightly higher than the sheet end. One way of checking that the clews are level is to look at the centerline seam of the sail. If it is vertical, the sail is set well and drawing easily.

Third, the pole should be horizontal. If the pole slants upward or downward, less area is being projected into the wind. Figure 26-2 shows how the spinnaker area diminishes if the pole is improperly set.

If you obey those three rules, trimming the spinnaker is easy. Ease the sheet until the luff has a slight curl. When the curl

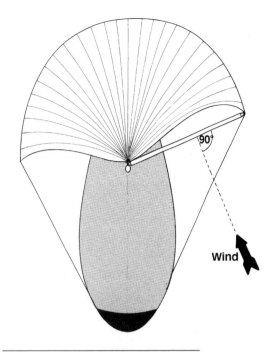

Figure 26-1: Set the spinnaker pole at right angles to the wind direction for maximum performance.

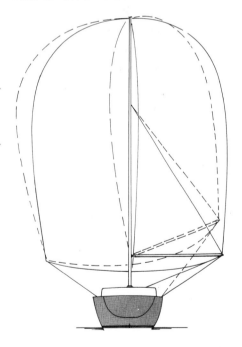

Figure 26-2: Set the spinnaker pole horizontal and at the same height as the leeward clew to maximize sail performance.

gets too large, trim in the sheet, and if the curl vanishes, ease the sheet. If you have to ease the sheet a lot, check to see if the pole should be pulled aft. Conversely, if you have to trim an excessive amount, move the pole forward.

Telltales on the pole can indicate where the wind is coming from, as do telltales on the luff and the leech of the spinnaker. I find it easier to keep an eye on the sail luff and the masthead indicator.

27: Setting and Trimming a Cruising Spinnaker

Cruising chutes are even easier to set than regular spinnakers because they do not need to be set on the end of the pole. Most cruising spinnakers are either a full-bellied genoa or a cross between a spinnaker and genoa. They can be tacked at the bow and sheeted to a guy well aft of the genoa sheet, or tacked to a spinnaker pole with the sheet taken well aft.

Leave the genoa set as the boat heads offwind. Fit the tack of the cruising spinnaker into the genoa tack fitting. Note that many cruising spinnakers have a short length of line to keep the sail from chafing on the lifeline. If yours does, hook the end of the line through the tack fitting. Tie on the sheet and lead it aft through a quarter block to a winch. Now hook in the halyard (if the halyard has been stowed at the mast, it will need to be led around the headstay or around the back of the headsail) and hoist away. With the sail hoisted in the lee of the genoa it should not fill and get away from you.

Once the cruising spinnaker is set, drop the genoa and trim the spinnaker like a normal downwind sail. Be careful that you do not let too much sheet out, or the luff will curl inward. If the sheet is overtight, the leech will often curl inward and cause the sail to collapse. By playing the leech and luff of the sail, you will find the position where it provides the best boat speed. Note that if you are going to run dead downwind with a cruising spinnaker, the tack can be put on a spinnaker pole or moved to the windward rail, which gets more of the sail out from behind the lee of the mainsail. You also might want to experiment with lowering the mainsail. On one boat we found that dropping the main allowed the spinnaker to draw better and resulted in better boat speed.

28: Reefing

If your method of reefing is simply to drop the mainsail and tie in the reef points, you can learn some things that will preserve the life of your mainsail and give you better boat speed and control of the boat.

In general, sails become fuller as the wind increases. That is, the belly of the sail deepens, the flow moves aft, and the leech tends to tighten up. All these factors increase the heel angle of the boat and reduce the speed. To get the best out of your boat you should flatten the mainsail as the wind increases. This is best done by taking up on the halyard and pulling the outhaul out. When the wind becomes heavier, the next step is to take up on the Cunningham eye and then put in the flattening reef. Depending on the boat, you may have to furl or change the headsail as well.

As the wind continues to increase in strength, the next step is to take in a reef. Make sure the reef lines are rigged properly. The line should run out from inside the boom to a turning block just aft of the present clew. (You need to pull the reef outward as well as downward to tension the sail foot.) From the block, the line should go through the reefing eye on the sail and back down to the boom, where it is tied off. If you have to tie the reef line around the boom, use a fisherman's bend, as shown in Figure 28-1. This will ensure the knot can be untied when the reef needs to be taken out. It, too, should be tied just aft of the clew.

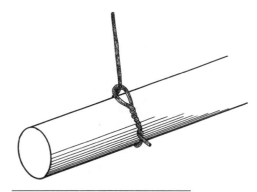

Figure 28-1: Use a fisherman's bend to tie the reefing line around the boom. This will make it easy to untie when the reef line is taken out.

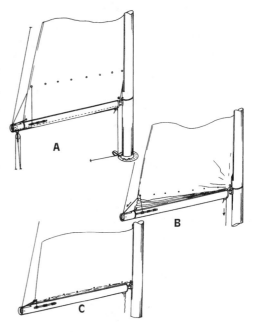

Figure 28-2: (A) The sail is full. (B) The halyard is eased and the luff is pulled down until it can be hooked on the reefing horn at the inboard end of the boom. The clew line is then pulled down. (C) Shows the entire reef taken in and the reefing line cleated off.

To reef, first ease the mainsheet, and then take up on the clew line. Tighten the clew line down until the clew of the reef is two-blocked. Then ease the halyard and put the tack ring over the horn on the gooseneck fitting (or reposition the pin if you have an older type gooseneck fitting). Now take up on the halyard again and sheet in. This is the basic reef. If you want the boat to sail more efficiently, you should tie in the reef lines all the way along the sail. (Remember not to tie in the mainsheet if it runs under the boom.) Reef points will make the belly of the sail flatter as well as hold the reef snugly (see Figure 28-2).

Finally, take the halyard back up and tighten it. Now take up on the mainsheet. The sail should be flat and ready for use. To take up a second reef, the operation is repeated and the reef tack is taken down to the horn on the other side of the boom.

29: Roller-Furling Sails

True or false: Roller-furling jibs and genoas are different from normal headsails. The answer is true, they are different. The material used in roller-furling headsails has to be durable and reasonably compact so that the sail can be rolled easily into a tight furl. It also should have good protection from ultraviolet rays, either over the entire sail or as a UV-protecting leach strip that shades the entire sail when it is furled.

Another useful feature on a roller-furled headsail is a foam luff patch that prevents the sail from bagging in the middle when it is reefed. (In the old days of boom-roller reefing, we used to stuff sail bags in the reef. Unfortunately, the crew rarely remembered when it was time to unroll the reef, and many races were finished with bagless sails piled on the cabin sole.) Using the roller-furled sail in a reefed position poses several problems, not the least of which is that shape is usually poor in any position other than fully unrolled. This means that the wise sailor will not attempt to use the sail with an arbitrary number of rolls in it. Ideally, you should set the sail up unrolled and position the headsail fairlead carefully. Then find a second position where, say, 10 percent of the sail is rolled in, and a third position where 20 percent of the sail is rolled in. Mark the foot of the sail to show how much is rolled up and *reposition the sheet lead* for each position. The lead will change for every roll you take up. Mark the position of the sheet lead on the track or deck and you will be ready to use the roller-furled headsail in a reefed position.

When using a roller-furled headsail, the most common problem is one of not enough headstay tension. Too loose a headstay will make the sail too full, making the boat heel more and sail slowly. This problem is exacerbated when the sail is reefed. Tightening the headstay will make the sail look much better under every condition and help the boat sail to windward better. The second most common problem is one of using a furling system that will not furl properly when the halyard or sheet is under load. If you are about to buy a furling system, check around carefully for one that is easy to maintain and operate. It should also be easily moveable under tension.

30: The Staysail

Staysails used to be set under all kinds of sails. I have used a mizzen staysail, a spinnaker staysail, and a genoa staysail. Today, with the advent of roller-furling, few staysails are set unless a yacht is purposely set up with a double-headsail rig.

Staysails, however, can enhance performance. A staysail set under a spinnaker not only fills the gap under the chute, it can also add additional power to the mainsail when the slot between the main and staysail is set up carefully.

If your boat has a mizzen mast, the mizzen staysail is another sail that adds power. On boats around 40 feet overall, the mizzen staysail can add up to a ¼ knot of additional speed. On a broad reach, the luff of the sail is generally set from the mizzen masthead to a tack padeye somewhere along the windward side of the yacht. The sheet may be taken to the yacht's quarter or to the end of the mizzen boom. (Note that if it is taken to the end of the mizzen boom, oversheeting should be avoided at all costs.)

As the wind comes forward, the staysail tack should be moved more toward the centerline. This means that the main boom must either be well ahead of the mizzen or eased sufficiently so that it will not interfere with the sail. If the boom touches the staysail, the staysail should be taken down.

A spinnaker staysail can be used in much the same fashion as a mizzen staysail. It can be tacked to windward on a broad reach and the tack moved toward the centerline as the wind comes ahead. However, when setting a spinnaker staysail, try to make sure that the leech of the sail complements the airflow on the leeward side of the mainsail. Its primary function should be to remove stalled air from the back of the mainsail and provide more driving power.

A genoa staysail, on the other hand, serves a slightly different purpose. It is generally used as part of a double-headed rig, where the headsail is a high cut Yankee or topsail. In this situation, the staysail provides a second slot between the headsail and the main, thus enhancing the airflow across both sails and increasing the available power. This means that its position should be carefully considered. If it is too far forward, it will hurt the airflow over the topsail, and if it is too far aft, it will hurt the mainsail airflow. About 35 to 40 percent of the distance from the forestay to the mast appears to be about right.

A sailmaker gave me this very rough guide to setting staysails. Set them at 5, 5, and 5. In other words, sheet the headsail in until it is drawing properly, then set the staysail 5 degrees lower and the mainsail 5 degrees lower than that. If a mizzen staysail is fitted, it should be set 5 degrees lower than the mainsail. Following this rule, it quickly becomes apparent that to use a mizzen staysail the boat cannot be close hauled, but must be on a reach. Setting staysails, then, is an arcane art, but one every sailor who wants to improve boat performance should master.

31: The Mizzen

I'm often asked if it is worth having a mizzen mast on a small boat. For boats under 40 feet, my reply usually is no. The reason mizzen masts have stayed popular on larger boats is that they allow the sail area to be broken up into easily handled segments.

Today, mizzen masts have a place on cruising boats that are not intended for extensive windward work. They offer several advantages in addition to breaking up sail area. A mizzen mast increases sail area for no gain in mast height; a mizzen staysail can be set on it; and it provides a good place to support the aft end of an awning. Should you lose the mainmast far out at sea, the mizzen can serve as a get-you-home mast, or as a sheer leg to help raise the spinnaker pole. If the mizzen is fairly small, as on a yawl, it can be set to serve as a weather vane to keep the bow of the boat into the wind in a hot climate.

When a boat designer sizes the mizzen mast, he generally assumes that it will not be used when sailing to windward, because a mizzen would have to be sheeted in too tightly to be effective. But as soon as the wind comes slightly aft, the mizzen sail can be used. This means it will probably be hoisted and lowered much more often than the mainsail, making it essential that the halyard and sheet are easy to operate.

Sheeting and using the mizzen is just like using the mainsail, except that the sail will be set about 5 degrees lower than the main. It should be reefed in the same manner, and can be fitted with lazy jacks or roller furling, just like the main and headsails. If you decide that your next boat should have a mizzen mast, its operation is just like the mainsail, except when sailing to windward.

32: Setting Storm Sails

Setting storm sails is something not every sailor longs to do, but knowing how to do it can save your life if you are caught in a severe gale.

The Storm Jib

Storm jibs are usually small. Some sailors say they are smaller than a pocket handkerchief, by way of saying that the wind has to be blowing pretty hard before they will use one. Storm jibs are usually made of heavyweight Dacron and strongly reinforced at each corner. They should be hanked on, because this is the only sure-fire method of keeping sails attached to the headstay in severe weather. I have heard it suggested that the sail be set in the luff groove and then laced to the headstay, but having been on the pointy end during a tropical storm with winds over 70 knots, I know that I would not want to spend the time lacing a line through grommets when the boat is ploughing through headseas.

To ensure the sail can be set correctly, try it out in harbor. After all, there is no point in getting into a good blow only to find that the padeye for the tack of the sail hasn't been fitted. If you set it in harbor, make sure the sail can be sheeted absolutely flat. (It will have plenty of curvature when you use it!) Also check to see how far the sail extends up the headstay. If the sail is fairly short, you might want to have a wire pennant made to take the strain off the halyard.

In order to keep the sailplan compact in heavy weather, consider fitting the storm jib on the midstay instead of on the headstay. If you want to do this, discuss the option with your sailmaker and boat builder before moving the sail. The sail may need to be cut differently and the deck may need to be reinforced around the midstay.

The Storm Trysail

The storm trysail is slightly different from the jib. Trysails are usually fitted in the mainsail luff groove, which means that to set the trysail you must be able to either lower or remove the mainsail. One of the older methods is to fit a second track and have a track gate, but most of today's sailors remove the mainsail completely and run under bare poles in a storm. Note, however, that running with a storm jib and no mainsail can lead to mast failure from the headsail compression on the mast without a compensating mainsail force on the back of the mast.

The clew of the trysail is usually taken to a position on the deck, or occasionally to the end of the boom. More often, the outer end of the boom is lashed down on deck. Note that the sail must be cut so that the clew can be sheeted correctly. Again, the position of the trysail should be tried out in harbor before you get out in the ocean in a severe blow.

Few boats today are fitted with a trysail track, and those that are, rarely use it. Many contemporary cruisers have roller-furling on both the mainsail and the headsail, and in a severe blow simply furl the main. Others, reluctant to sail in heavy winds, keep a careful eye on the weather forecast and pick their breeze. If you intend to cruise offshore for any length of time, however, you will eventually run into bad weather and should have provision for carrying a trysail.

Going Cruising

H ow do you plan a cruise? If you are the sailor whose planning is limited to finding the nearest place for liquid provisions and food, this section is for you. Here we'll look at planning the cruise, getting under way, sailing short-handed, and getting into the dock without relying on outside help.

How often have you been on a cruise and found that you needed something? If this happens to you often enough, you haven't organized your cruise properly.

If you plan to cruise in unfamiliar waters, the first requirement will be up-to-date charts. Select charts for the route, for your destination, and one or two for harbors along the way, in case the weather turns bad and you have to find a safe haven.

Spread out the charts and figure out how far your boat can sail in the time you want to spend sailing every day. Let's say that your boat cruises at six knots and you want to sail about six or seven hours a day. That gives you a range of 36 to 42 miles each day. Remember to include time for locks or opening bridges; quite often these open only at set times. You should allow one or two days for bad weather and for sightseeing, so in your two weeks of sailing you will probably not want to range much further than 150 to 200 miles from your base. If you wander much further, you may have to push hard to get the boat home, and pushing hard always seems to be a step away from disaster. I remember a trip where we simply had to move a boat on the south coast of England from Portland to Gosport. We waited for the winds to pick up rather than motoring in the calms that were forecast. Finally, we had only two days to make the trip and it blew a full gale on both days. We left in a gale and arrived in a gale, and were lucky nothing went wrong.

After you have figured out how far your trip will range, check the tide tables and estimate when you are likely to pass areas of major tidal streams. For instance, the tidal stream in the Race at the eastern end of Long Island Sound runs at speeds up to six knots, and in parts of the English Channel there are tides of up to nine knots. It will take you a long time to get through this narrow channel if you enter when the tide is running against you. Try to pass areas like this when the tide is flowing with you. Once you have determined the ideal time to pass such areas, you can work backward and calculate the time you should leave the home dock.

Having laid out your route and your arrival and departure times and locations, check with each marina you will stop in to make sure they have vacancies. If you will be swinging on your own anchor overnight, check that all parts of your ground tackle are in good shape. A frayed anchor line at the beginning of the cruise can turn into a broken line after five nights of anchoring.

When your cruise itinerary is set, give a copy of it to a trusted person on shore. When you have arrived at one of your destinations, it is a simple matter to telephone that person and confirm that you are proceeding on schedule, or let the person know about any departures from your itinerary. If you are overdue, that person can alert the authorities.

If a harbor you are going to visit has a port directory or local yacht club, you may want to check and see if there are local facilities, such as a laundry, supermarket, chandlery, power outlets, fresh water, a mechanic in case something goes wrong with your mechanical systems, or even travel-lift facilities in case you have to haul the boat. Another useful item is a guidebook for an area where you might want to do some sightseeing, or a foreign language dictionary if another language is spoken there. These books will help make your stay more interesting and can help entertain your children, as well as interest them in the local area. If you have school-age children you might suggest they research places of interest in the ports you are going to visit.

Even the best plans can go astray if your provisioning is not done right. If you are planning a two- or three-week cruise, inventory the galley and find out exactly what food, drink, dishes, and utensils you have aboard. Also check to see what pots and pans you have. It is no use buying lobsters for a special meal if you don't have a pot to cook them in.

Having made your inventory, inquire about the food preferences of your crew. When you are barbecuing a thick steak you don't want to suddenly discover that two of your crew members are vegetarians. Some skippers have a form letter that they send to all new crew members. This letter suggests what gear to bring along and asks about food and other preferences.

Now you can make out your shopping list. Remember to include ample soft drinks, crackers, and "casual foods." In my experience, few people want the bother of cooking a large meal in the stifling confines of a yacht's galley every evening. Also remember that if you buy meats, they should be frozen before putting them on board. This will slow their deterioration and help to lower the temperature in the icebox.

If you are super-organized and want to have maximum free time on your cruise, make up a batch of frozen meals, such as casseroles or lasagna, that can be popped into the oven when required. Served with a green salad and bread, the entire meal will take just a few minutes to prepare, leaving time to enjoy a lazy swim or a trip ashore.

Don't forget such items as cleaning products, toilet paper, and kitchen towels. You will also need garbage bags in which to store your trash until it can be disposed of properly ashore. Even if you have holding tanks, buy a biodegradable toilet roll, and make sure it will not clog the WC. Nobody wants to spend their vacation disassembling the head.

34: Going-to-Sea Checklist

The items listed here are in addition to the usual life jackets, harnesses, and safety gear that a yacht would normally carry.

WHAT TO BRING FOR A SHORT CRUISE

Adequate provisions for the duration of the cruise, plus a few additional cans of food in case the trip takes longer than estimated:

    First aid kit, plus sunscreen and sunburn lotion
    Fishing tackle, if desired
    Matches
    Flares
    Charts for all harbors
    Fresh water (assume one gallon per person per day)
    Spare batteries for all battery-operated items
    Spare navigation lights
    Extra changes of clothes in case the weather turns nasty
    Foghorn (with extra cylinders if gas-powered)
    Foul weather gear and sailing (waterproof) boots
    Fire extinguisher(s)
    Dinghy (with pump, repair kit, oars, bailer, bottom boards, painter, towline)
    Outboard (with fuel and oil, spare plug(s), padlock and chain to secure outboard)

MECHANICAL AND ELECTRICAL EQUIPMENT CHECKS

Perform these checks a few days before your cruise starts:
    Check fuel level

Check engine oil and coolant levels

Check batteries

Check that all navigation lights are working properly

Check alternators to make sure they are charging

Check engine belts for wear and replace if worn

Check that all through-hull fittings operate properly and are not frozen or badly worn

Make sure that all your electronic instruments are working. If the radar and depth gauge have been malfunctioning, get them fixed and test them before departure

ON DECK

Check the mast from top to bottom. Look at wear on the sheaves and boxes. Check the spreader roots for cracks

Check all rigging and remove meathooks or replace the wire

Check the lifelines for signs of corrosion and replace if rusty

Pull the sails off the boat and have a sailmaker look them over

Check all the mechanical gear on deck for signs of binding, wear, and corrosion. Replace or refit as needed

Check that the cockpit drains work properly

Check that you have storm boards for large windows, and that you have a method of fastening the storm boards

Check that the boarding ladder is in good shape

Check the anchor line, anchor, shackles, and mousings

Check the stemhead for sharp edges that might cut your anchor line

Check that the emergency steering works

Review emergency procedures with crew

ADDITIONAL ITEMS TO BRING FOR A LONGER CRUISE

A life raft capable of holding the entire crew

Flares/distress signals

Extra fresh water in containers

Extra food

Storm coverings

Storm sails

Tools (hacksaw, wrenches, bolt cutters, screwdrivers)

Ship's bell

Charts for all areas that you may pass through

Compasses (check they have been swung recently)

Adequate spare fuel or a plan for obtaining it

Traveler's checks/cash/credit cards

Passport/Visa

The wind is rising and the seas are getting bigger. You have another 30 hours of sailing before you reach a safe haven. What do you do? Following are some precautions you can take to make your boat safer and more comfortable if you anticipate heavy weather.

The first step is to prepare. Make a batch of sandwiches and put them in sealed plastic bags. Make a hot drink and put it in a vacuum flask to keep it warm. You may not have time to do this later.

Issue plastic bags to all the crew so they can store their dry clothing and make sure the bags are sealed with a twist tie. Give out additional bags for wet clothing. I rarely bother to change out of wet gear during a storm, as the new clothes quickly get wet, but as soon as the storm has abated, dry clothes are a real tonic.

Carefully check your position and the direction of the storm, and set a course to avoid being caught on the wrong side of it. If the oncoming storm is a hurricane with circular winds and you are sailing in the northern hemisphere, set a course to take you to the westward side of the storm, where the wind velocity is slightly lower (see Figure 35-1). Make sure you have plenty of sea room if the storm forecast is for a severe gale.

If the storm is likely to be a moderate gale, your precautions can be moderate as well. Make sure that all crew members have harnesses, and that they know where the life jackets are. In fact, you might want to give each crewman a life jacket to try on and learn to inflate. If the yacht has jacklines or safety ropes running down the deck, make sure that the crew knows to clip on before leaving the safety of the cockpit. Make sure the crew also knows where the man-overboard life ring, pole, drogue, and strobe light are and how they operate.

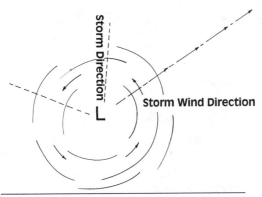

Figure 35-1: The winds on the storm's western (left) side are slightly lower than the winds on the east (right) side. On the east side the storm's forward velocity is added to the speed of the wind in the storm. On the west side, the speed of the wind is reduced by the speed of the storm's forward motion.

If a severe storm is forecast, find the storm boards for all large openings, in case a hatch or large window shatters when the sea hits it. Put the storm boards up before the wind grows too strong. Remove any leecloths, awnings, biminis, or other canvas that can get blown away. If you have an inflatable dinghy lashed to the cabin top, you might want to deflate it and stow it in a locker so that it will not be blown away. If your dinghy is rigid, make sure it is securely fastened down with extra lashings. Take small items such as oars, fenders, and lines below deck or stow them in a locker for the duration of the storm; they could become missiles in strong winds. Double-lash the life raft to make sure it doesn't blow away. If the yacht is in trouble, you can cut the lashings quickly with a sharp knife.

Make sure the boat's hatches can be closed securely. You might want to install one or two washboards and leave the top of the companionway open until the storm gets strong. Close all the hatches if the storm increases in intensity. Also make sure that any crew members prone to sea sickness take their pills or apply wristbands or patches.

Make sure the storm sails are immediately to hand. On one trip to Bermuda our storm trysail was at the bottom of the companionway hatch waiting to be used, while the storm jib was doing its job at the front of the boat. Other handy items for on-deck wear are a pair of swimming goggles (or scuba mask), which will help you look to windward in heavy spray and wind. A hat with a large brim, tied securely to your head, will help keep water from running down your neck.

36: Leaving the Dock

The engine revs and the boat strains against the spring lines. The bow swings in toward the walkway as the stern line is thrown off. A crew member tries to stop the bow from grinding on the dock. The owner, seeing the impending crash, throws the gear shift from full ahead to full astern in one swift motion. Water boils under the transom as the prop tries to keep pace with the owner's demands. The bow line is thrown off, followed by a spring. Then the other spring is let go and the boat thrusts out of the dock, bouncing off a piling on the way. The crewman who threw off the lines is standing on the marina walkway, wondering how to get aboard.

Sound familiar? We've all had a similar experience in our sailing lifetime, and with any luck we have learned from it.

Leaving a marina berth can be a painless operation if the crew follows a few simple rules. The first and most important rule is to take it easy. Rarely should the engine be run at full speed; slamming the gear shift from full ahead to full astern without pausing to let the prop stop spinning can result in costly repairs to the engine and transmission.

You should know which way the stern will swing when the prop is put astern. Usually the stern will swing to port. If you are moored port side to, you will have to get the stern away from the berth wall before going astern. The simplest and least glamorous way is to have your crew push the boat off. Another way is shown in Figures 36-1A and 36-1B. The bow and stern lines are cast off, as is the aft-leading spring, leaving one spring (A). When the rudder is turned to port and engine revs *gently* increased, the bow will swing toward the dock. Note the strategically placed fender at the bow. From here it is a simple matter to put the engine astern and cast off the spring line as soon as the load comes off it. You can then back the boat out of the marina in the usual way.

If the boat is tied up starboard side to and the stern kicks to port when going astern, the job is simpler: let the stern go where it wants to, but keep a fender ready at the bow in case it comes too close to the dock.

If you are moored alongside a dock wall between other boats, the technique of springing as illustrated in Figures 36-1A and 36-1B can be used to get the stern out into clear water. Note also that if several boats are rafted up astern of you, the same maneuver can be used to get the bow clear (see Figure 36-2). If it is difficult to get clear because there are boats moored fore and aft of you, you may be able to use a nearby piling or dock, or even a breast anchor, to pull the boat out of its slot. In Figure 36-3A, a line has been taken to a piling abreast of the boat. The springs are removed and the bow and stern lines eased to enable the crew to pull the boat out of its berth. With the boat moored between piling and berth the sails are made ready, and the jib hoisted, as shown in Figure 36-3B. As soon as the jib is drawing, the mooring lines can be let go and the boat proceeds out of the harbor. If you don't want to set the sails, the lines can be let go as soon as the motor is running.

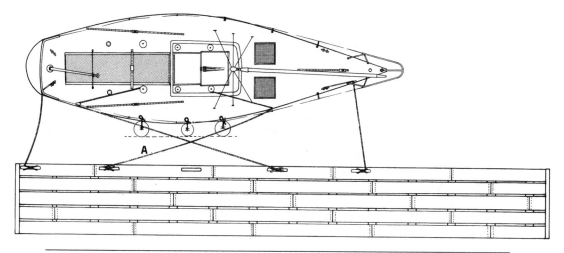

Figure 36-1A: The boat is sitting at the dock with all lines on board. The aft leading spring (A) is the only one that will not be removed.

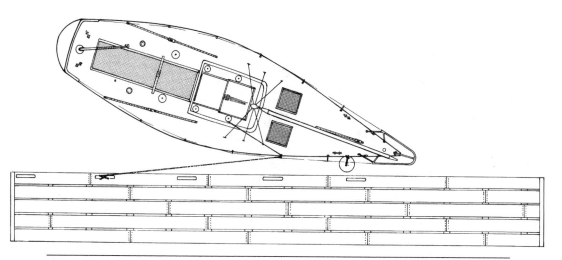

Figure 36-1B: Using the spring, the boat is motored slowly ahead. Note that the rudder is turned to bring the bow in. A well placed fender is ready to prevent any contact between boat and dock. As soon as the stern has swung out, the propeller is reversed and the boat backed away from the dock.

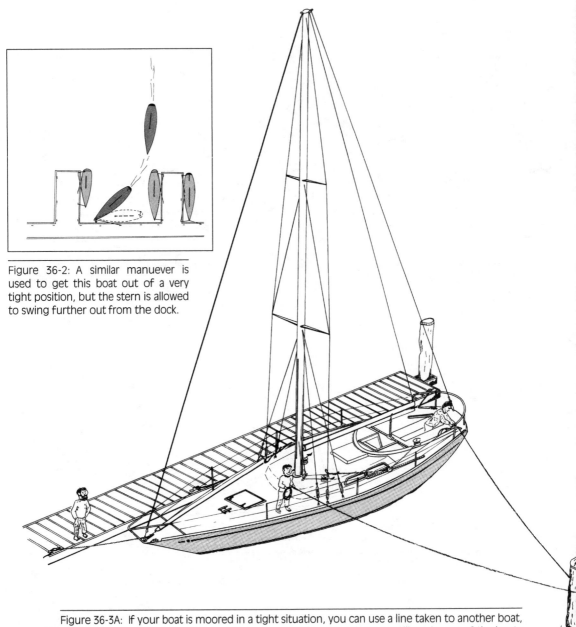

Figure 36-2: A similar manuever is used to get this boat out of a very tight position, but the stern is allowed to swing further out from the dock.

Figure 36-3A: If your boat is moored in a tight situation, you can use a line taken to another boat, a piling, or a dock to get you out easily. Here a line has been taken to a piling abreast of the boat.

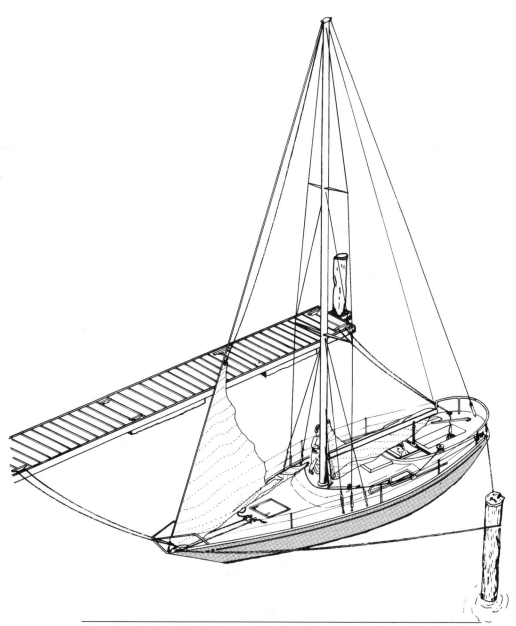

Figure 36-3B: The spring lines are removed and the bow and stern lines eased to enable the crew to pull the boat out of its berth.

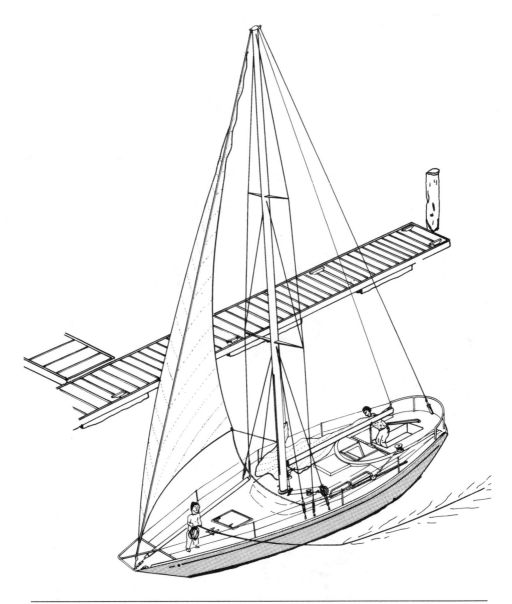

Figure 36-3C. With the boat moored between piling and berth the engine is turned on, or the sails are made ready, and the jib hoisted. As soon as the jib is drawing or the engine is put in gear, the mooring lines are let go and the boat proceeds out of the harbor.

37: Leaving a Mooring

You've stowed the food, put away the crew bags, and made the sails ready. Now you are about to get under way. Many sailors think leaving a mooring buoy under power is easy—you simply drop the pennant and put the engine in gear. Right?

Wrong! If you lose sight of the buoy you may motor over it and get the pennant tangled in the prop, which will turn your nice cruise into an embarrassing swim in the middle of the mooring field. When you cast off the mooring line, the person casting off should stand in the bow and indicate which way the buoy lies until the helmsman can see it clearly.

Leaving a buoy under sail is slightly more difficult. Usually the moored boat will lie pointing into the wind. This means that before you can get underway you will have to swing the boat's head out of the eye of the wind. Putting the jib aback shortly after casting off the mooring line will usually accomplish this. Note that you will need room for the boat to drift downwind with the jib aback before you will be able to tack the jib and get underway.

Figures 37-1A, B, C, and D show the sequence of events. In Figure 37-1A, the boat is hanging on its mooring and the mainsail is hoisted but not sheeted in. In B, the mooring is about to be dropped and the mainsail backed. Note the direction the rudder is pointing. The idea is to get the bow to fall off to port as soon as possible. Note also that the mainsail should not yet be sheeted fully in. It is best to trim the main just enough so that the boat will start moving ahead. In C, the rudder has been centered, the mainsail is now set and drawing, and the headsail is being hoisted. The idea at this stage, D, is to get the boat moving. Usually this is accomplished by keeping the boat on a reach and hardening up later.

Getting under way without using the motor is a rewarding task and one that you should master. One day, you may find that your engine will not start and you have to sail the boat into the dock in order to get it fixed. A few practice sessions, with the motor running in neutral in case of emergency, will greatly improve your confidence when a real challenge presents itself.

Figure 37-1A, B, C, D: In A the boat is hanging on a mooring and the mainsail is hoisted but not sheeted in. In B, the mooring is about to be dropped and the mainsail backed. Note which way the rudder has been pointed. The idea is to get the bow to fall to port as soon as possible. Note also that the mainsail has not yet been sheeted fully in. It is best to trim the main just enough so that the boat will start moving ahead. In C, the rudder has been centered, the headsail is being hoisted, and the mainsail is being trimmed. In D, the idea is to get the boat moving. Usually this is accomplished by keeping the boat on a reach and hardening up later.

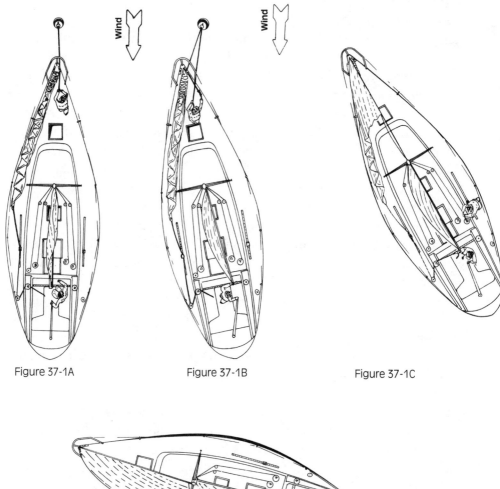

Figure 37-1A   Figure 37-1B   Figure 37-1C

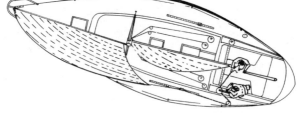

Figure 37-1D

38: Setting Sail

Setting sail is a task you do every time you go sailing, and it should be so straightforward that it hardly needs explanation. But setting sail to get the best out of your sails with a minimum of flogging takes a little more skill.

First, make sure the boom is supported by the vang or topping lift, and ease the mainsheet. Remove all the sail ties (even experts often forget the ties until the sail is halfway up) and hook up the halyard. Make sure the halyard shackle is screwed up tightly, and check aloft to ensure that the halyard is not twisted around other halyards or mast fittings. Now the sail is ready to be hoisted.

The helmsman should bring the boat into the wind. His sole job is to keep the boat head-to-wind. A crew member raises the halyard, checking, as he does so, that the sail is not caught or snagged on its way aloft. When the sail is fully hoisted, use binoculars to check if the top of the sail is against the black band (if you have them) or tensioned to suit the wind strength. If not, cleat the sail temporarily and sheet in to check the sail shape. If the wind is strong, take up on the outhaul and the halyard a little more. If the wind is light, you might need to ease them.

Adjust the halyard until there are no vertical creases in the sail (caused by having the halyard too tight) and no horizontal creases (caused by having the halyard too slack). If the lower part of the sail is very deep, pull the outhaul out, do *not* introduce horizontal creases. If the sail is full in the middle third and the outhaul is just right, you may require a little mast bend. Refer back to Section 4 for details on sail control.

Having set the mainsail without the complication of a headsail, you can now set the genoa or jib. Hoist it or unroll it and check the sheet angles (described in Section 4, Chapter 23). Note that it often helps to keep a slight tension on the furling line as the sail is being unrolled. This reduces the sail's ability to flog, which degrades the stitching.

At this point you'll probably find that the mainsail is backwinded; that is, there is a bubble in the forward part of the sail. This is a simple problem. Set the boom on the centerline by raising the traveler; tighten the outhaul and sheet until the bubble almost disappears and the telltales stream aft correctly. How much you adjust them will vary according to the boat and the weather conditions.

The genoa also will need some adjustment. First check the luff of the sail.

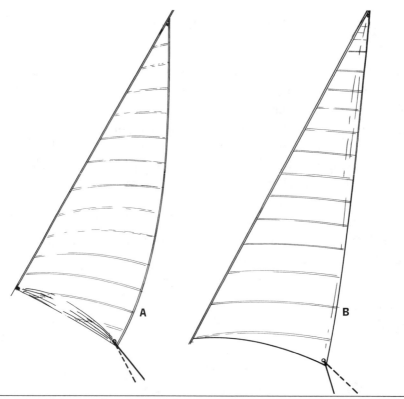

Figure 38-1: If there are lines along the foot of the headsail (A), ease the sheet and move the sheet lead forward a hole or two (B). This has the effect of rounding the foot and making the sail more powerful in light winds or conditions where a heavy sea is running.

Are there vertical or horizontal lines? Tightening the halyard will remove horizontal lines and easing the halyard will remove vertical lines. If you have lines along the foot, ease the sheet and move the sheet lead forward, as shown in Figure 38-1.

39: Self-Tacking Methods

Rather than straining away at the winches when tacking, set your boat up so that tacking can be accomplished by simply turning the wheel or pushing the rudder. To do this, the mainsheet and the jib must have their own tracks. It also precludes the use of a large, overlapping genoa.

Figure 39-1A shows the track position for a self-tacking jib. Note that it runs transversely across the boat just forward of the mast. The jib clew can be sheeted directly to this track without a club-foot boom. For windward work, this is quite suitable, but sailing on a reach, the jib may get sucked in behind the mainsail and lose efficiency. For this reason, a club-foot boom is often fitted.

Should you decide to use a boom, it will need somewhere to pivot. Several manufacturers make a pedestal; one design I saw on a fairly large boat incorporated a dorade-type vent in the unit, and another was part of the anchor windlass support. If you decide you do not want a pedestal, some booms have a special attachment that can be bolted to the headstay just below the luff groove, but a club-foot boom should be high enough to clear the lifelines when the yacht is running downwind (see Figure 39-1B).

The sheeting arrangement is reasonably simple: stops on either end of the track hold the tack car at the required spacing. On all except larger vessels, the sheet is a single-part line led forward from the track to a block on the centerline and then aft to the winch or lock off.

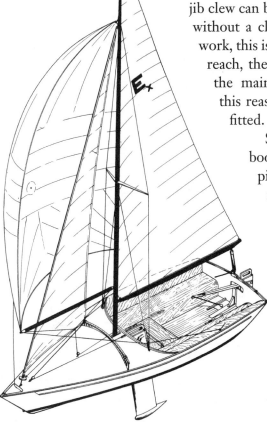

Figure 39-1A: The track position for a self-tacking jib is just in front of the mast, as shown in this dinghy designed by the author.

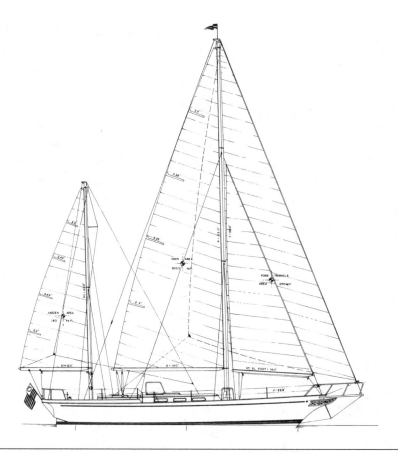

Figure 39-1B: This author-designed ketch has a boomed staysail with a track just forward of the mainmast. Note that the boom is high enough to clear the lifelines.

40: Picking Up a Mooring Under Sail

You've had a nice cruise and you are returning to the mooring. Most sailors take their sails down long before they get to the mooring buoy and pick up the buoy under power. Should your engine fail, however, it's helpful to know how to pick up the mooring under sail. The first step is to ascertain which direction the wind and tide are coming from, and whether the wind is with the tide, against the tide, or across the tide. In Figure 40-1, the wind and tide are moving in the same direction. To get to the mooring buoy requires a fine eye and attention to detail. The approach should be slightly upwind but across the

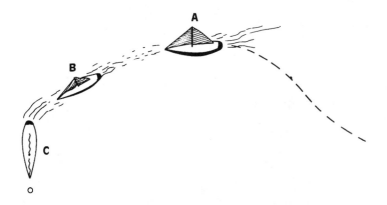

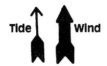
Tide Wind

Figure 40-1: When approaching a buoy under sail with wind and tide from the same direction, the idea is to stay just to windward of the buoy until the last moment. Then dip to leeward, ease the mainsail and headsail (A), and shoot up toward the buoy (B). If you time it right you will reach the buoy just as the boat speed has dropped to a crawl (C). Drop the sails as soon as the mooring line is aboard and secure.

wind and tide. The intention is to maintain a slight windward gauge on the buoy until the last few boat lengths. At that time, the boat will duck downwind and downtide of the buoy, round up, and carry its way right to the buoy. Note that you can sail under main or jib or both sails, but remember that you will sail slower and make more leeway under a single sail.

In Figure 40-2, the boat is at position A, upwind of the buoy and uptide of it. The approach can be made from any angle until the boat reaches point B, where the mainsail is dropped and stowed as the boat heads toward the buoy under jib. Ease the jib until the boat speed has dropped to a crawl (C). As soon as the mooring pennant is on board, drop the jib.

In Figure 40-3, the boat is approaching the buoy with the wind at right angles to the tide direction. This approach takes a fine eye to gauge when to shoot up to the buoy. The ideal is to reach the buoy just as the tide pushes the boat down on it. In a strong tide the bow will be pointing above the buoy as the boat makes its turn. With moderate headway and the jib dropped on deck, the boat should coast up to the buoy and approach it just as speed falls to zero. The foredeck crew need to grab the mooring pennant quickly and get it aboard before the boat is swept downtide. I prefer to use a headsail for this approach, but many sailors like to use the main. As the boat nears the buoy, the headsail can

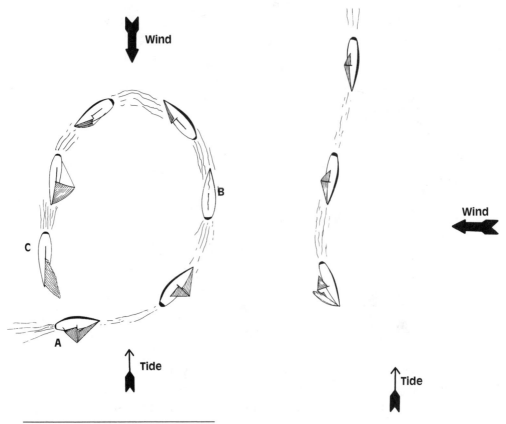

Figure 40-2: In this approach the wind and tide are running in opposite directions. The approach should be made upwind under jib. By varying the jib trim, the speed of the boat can be controlled, so that the approach is made very slowly. As soon as the mooring pennant has been picked up the headsail is dropped.

Figure 40-3: In this approach the wind is at right angles to the tide. The boat heads across the wind and against the tide. At the last moment, the boat is turned into the wind and the bow allowed to fall off to the buoy. In the initial turn the bow should be aimed above the buoy to allow the tide to push the bow toward it.

be dropped quickly, and the helmsman can still see forward. Often, if the mainsail is used and dropped as the buoy is to hand, the mainsail hides everything forward of the middeck.

Picking up a mooring under sail can be quite exciting, especially if any of the crew members miss their cues and there are spectators watching. Expect muttered comments if the foredeck crew is slow and the skipper has to go round again. If the buoy is missed a third time, the skipper generally exhibits a screaming temper tantrum.

41: Returning to Berth Under Power

Returning to the dock can be a tricky job if the tide is running strongly. Getting a boat alongside the dock, for example, when the tide is pushing the boat away from it is difficult even with the engine in use. The situation is equally tricky when the tide is pushing the boat onto the dock. Knowing your boat well can make a difference when docking. On most boats, the prop kicks the stern to port when the engine is put into reverse. This feature can make docking easier.

Docking when the tide is pushing the boat away from the dock requires some aggressive maneuvering. As Figure 41-1 shows, your intention should be to lay the bow alongside the dock, put the engine astern, and allow the kick of

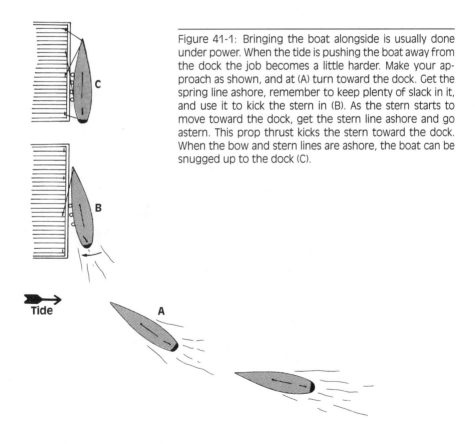

Figure 41-1: Bringing the boat alongside is usually done under power. When the tide is pushing the boat away from the dock the job becomes a little harder. Make your approach as shown, and at (A) turn toward the dock. Get the spring line ashore, remember to keep plenty of slack in it, and use it to kick the stern in (B). As the stern starts to move toward the dock, get the stern line ashore and go astern. This prop thrust kicks the stern toward the dock. When the bow and stern lines are ashore, the boat can be snugged up to the dock (C).

the prop to bring the stern in. At position A in Figure 41-1, the boat is making its approach to the dock. In B, the bow is turned to starboard and the dock line is thrown ashore. Allow plenty of slack in the dock line. The boat is still turned to starboard, and the engine kicked ahead. This should start bringing the stern in toward the dock. When the stern line is ashore the engine can be put astern. This should keep the stern moving toward the dock, and make it easy to take up on the stern line.

Should this operation fail and the stern line not land ashore, the bow line can be used as a spring and cleated off. The rudder should be turned to port and the engine put into half ahead. In theory, this will turn the bow away from the dock and allow the stern to swing into the dock.

If you must approach the dock from the other direction, you will not be able to use the prop thrust to drive the stern toward the dock. In this case, you must bring the bow in close to the mooring cleat. Get a line ashore and cleated off. Leave plenty of slack in the bow line to let the bow swing out. As the stern

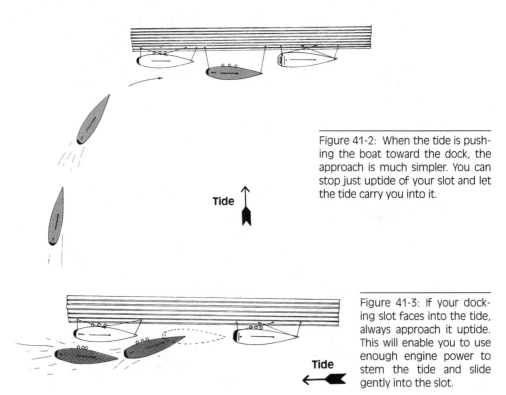

Tide

Figure 41-2: When the tide is pushing the boat toward the dock, the approach is much simpler. You can stop just uptide of your slot and let the tide carry you into it.

Tide

Figure 41-3: If your docking slot faces into the tide, always approach it uptide. This will enable you to use enough engine power to stem the tide and slide gently into the slot.

swings toward the dock, get the stern line ashore and cleated *before* going astern. The moment the engine is put astern, the stern will kick out and move further away from the dock. As soon as the stern line is ashore, the boat can be stopped and, if necessary, winched in tight to the dock.

If the tide is pushing the boat onto the dock, you can use this to your advantage. Don't worry about slick parking. Come to a stop about six to ten feet (2 to 3 meters) uptide of the dock space and let the tide carry you down to it, as shown in Figure 41-2. That way you will be able to adjust fenders and lines as the boat is drifting into its space. Note that you may have to rig a fender board to keep the hull away from pilings, and if the tide is particularly strong, you may have to set a breast anchor before drifting into your space. The fender board and breast anchor should be readied before the boat is put alongside, because when the tide is running, it can be difficult to push a boat far enough off the pilings to put a fender board in place.

When approaching a dock space with the tide running parallel to the boat's centerline, always try to approach uptide. In a downtide approach, your boat is moving at both the tide speed and your approach speed, which usually makes things happen extremely quickly. An uptide approach will enable you to move slowly into position. Run the engine at a slightly higher speed than normal to give you more maneuverability. Figure 41-3 shows an uptide approach. Quite often, in a fairly strong tide, you will be able to come alongside your berthing space and simply edge the boat sideways into the space.

42: Sailing into a Marina

Most boat owners return to their marina under engine, but occasionally you should try it under sail. If your engine fails, putting the boat alongside under sail requires skill and careful coordination. Practice the maneuver several times to make sure you can do it easily when necessary. Keep the engine running during your practice runs in case you get into trouble.

When wind and tide are moving in the same direction, it is best to approach the dock from the reach with either a main or jib alone. If both sails are up, the boat will be moving at close to maximum speed and you may not be able to stop quickly enough as you come alongside. I prefer to use the jib only, as it is easier and faster to drop as the boat nears the dock. Make the approach with

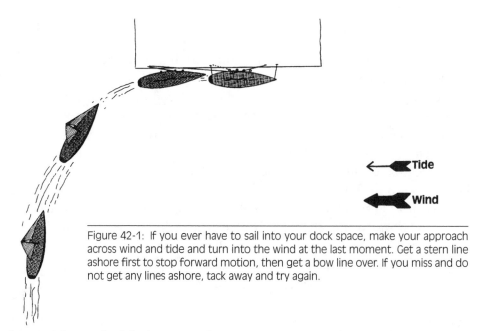

Tide

Wind

Figure 42-1: If you ever have to sail into your dock space, make your approach across wind and tide and turn into the wind at the last moment. Get a stern line ashore first to stop forward motion, then get a bow line over. If you miss and do not get any lines ashore, tack away and try again.

the wind forward of the beam, as shown in Figure 42-1, but *not* closehauled. If you approach closehauled, a header could force you to tack away because you cannot quite lay your dock space.

As the boat nears the dock space, ease the jib sheet to slow the vessel. If it looks as if you may not make the space, sheet in and pick up speed. As you near your space, drive off slightly and swing the boat up into the wind. If you time it right, you should arrive at the dock with very little way on and lines ready to be put ashore. If you miss, you will be able to come onto the other tack and sail away from the dock. This will give you time to get reorganized and make another approach.

If wind and tide are in opposing directions, the operation is slightly easier in that the tide will help slow the boat as you approach. The approach is similar to that described above: sail toward the dock on a close fetch.

With the tide at any other angle than dead ahead or dead astern, the problem becomes much easier. By trimming or easing sails, you can control boat speed, and by sailing uptide you can maneuver the boat up, down, or across the tide easily. A boat can be sailed into a dock simply by controlling speed under sail. In this situation, the sails are trimmed so that the boat just creeps uptide. Again, I prefer to use the jib alone, but some sailors prefer just the mainsail.

When docking under sail, the golden rule is simply *take your time*. Before the advent of mechanical power, boats often waited days for a favorable wind and tide. A few minutes of slow maneuvering will make up for hours spent sanding a gouge out of the topsides or toerail.

43: Did You Forget Your Car Keys?

How many times have you arrived at your boat only to find that you have forgotten your keys, or remembered that you left the forehatch open when you're halfway home? Often a quick call to the yard can solve your dilemma, but if the yard has closed and rain is forecast, you might have a messy clean-up before you can go sailing again.

Table 1 provides a list of things to do both before you leave the dock and before you leave to go home. Most of the items are simple things, but they are often forgotten in the rush to get sailing. Table 2 is a list of things to do if you are faced with a severe storm while the boat is moored or tied up at dockside. You might want to adapt these lists for your boat and post them prominently on board.

Table 1

On boarding the boat:
Stow the padlock and keys where they can be found.
Open the engine intake seacock before starting the engine. Note: Check the engine exhaust to make sure water is coming out after starting the engine.
Open the engine fuel line.
Check the bilges for seawater (and gas if the boat has a propane stove). Note: Do not smoke or use a match to check for gas.
Stow the companionway wash boards under the quarter berth (or wherever they are supposed to be stowed).
Check the stuffing box.
Untie the wheel or tiller before leaving the mooring.
Stick the ensign in its socket.

On leaving the boat:
Turn off the battery.
Turn off the gas at the tank.
Turn off the engine fuel.
Close the seacocks.

Close and lock the forehatch.

Take down the burgee and stow the ensign.

Fasten all the doors so that they cannot bang.

Fasten the halyards away from the mast.

Stow the dinghy, life raft, outboard, life rings, and anything else that might get stolen.

Leave the refrigerator/freezer door open.

Remove all the perishable food.

Open the vents where needed.

Lock the companionway. Make sure the keys are on your side of it.

Check that the mooring pennant is securely fastened and unlikely to chafe.

Table 2

If a storm is forecast, it makes good sense to take additional precautions:

Lay out additional ground tackle.

Double up on your mooring lines.

If your boat is on a mooring, add a second pennant fastened directly to the mooring line, instead of to the buoy.

Make sure all your chafing gear is in place.

Remove the roller-furled headsail, which might blow open and shred.

Remove the mainsail.

Remove the cockpit dodgers and leecloths.

Remove the life raft.

Fasten all halyards away from the mast.

Put the yacht's fenders out in case another vessel inadvertently comes alongside. (Fasten the fenders horizontally rather than vertically along the hull, so that another boat will bounce off.)

If the boat is alongside the dock, reposition it as near to the middle of the dock as possible so that fenders do not chafe or ride over the walkway.

Check with the owner of the boat in the next slip to see if a breast line between the boats will keep both vessels from riding up onto the marina walkway.

Check on your insurance policy to make sure it is fully paid.

Remove any valuables form the yacht (you might want to remove expensive electronics at the same time if the storm is forecast to be exceptionally severe).

Make sure that the dinghy, oars, and bailer are secure.

In a severe storm, such as a hurricane, it is best to haul your boat out of the water. Make sure you have the telephone number of a boatyard or someone who can haul your boat.

Find out about an available hurricane hole (a sheltered harbor or other location where your boat can ride out a storm safely) in case you cannot get your boat hauled.

If you have to use a hurricane hole, make sure you get there early.

Techniques

I n this section we'll look at the techniques used to operate a boat, including tacking, gybing, and changing sails. A tack, for instance, can be methodical and easy or disorganized, with several people trimming the winch while others stand back and yell. This type of tack not only slows the boat but also makes the crew tense, making it likely that another poor tack will follow. If each crewman knows his job and does it smartly and quickly, the boat will sail more efficiently and crew morale will rise.

44: Fully Crewed Tacking

"Lee ho!" the helmsman says, and the bow swings through the wind. The sheet is thrown off and pulled in on the other side, followed by winching. Fifteen minutes later the perspiring crew has finally pulled the sheet in far enough to allow the boat to be sailed close hauled. Does that sound like your boat? If so, you'll be pleased to know that you don't have to go through all that torture every time you tack. When tacking, the critical factor is timing—timing on the part of the helmsman, on the part of the crew throwing the sheet off, and on the part of the crew tailing the new sheet.

The helmsman's job is to warn everyone that the boat is about to be tacked. Usually this is done with the order, "stand by to go about." The following order, ("Helms alee" or "lee ho!") tells you that the tiller has been put down. With a cruising crew, the helmsman should make this a smooth operation without necessarily putting the rudder all the way to the stops. If the boat comes around slowly, it will be easier for the crew to throw off the old sheet and to pull in the new sheet before the sails are fully filled on the new tack. Also, by not slamming the rudder against the stops, water flow over the rudder blade stays attached and recovery from the tack is quicker.

At the "stand by" command, the crewman on the leeward side should remove the winch handle, unwrap the leeward sheet from its cleat, and remove all but three or four turns from the winch. He should also check that the sheet tail is free to run.

On the weather or windward side, another crewman should put two or three turns of the lazy sheet on the winch. Some tailers insert the winch handle at this time but my preference is to leave it out because it could fly out of its socket. The crewman should check that the sheet is not snagged on anything around the mast before announcing "Ready" to the helmsman.

As the boat comes into the wind, the lee side crewmember should ease the sheet a foot or two to move the leech forward of the spreader, and then watch the luff of the sail. When the sail starts to backwind, throw the sheet off entirely.

The crewmember who is tailing the new sheet on what is *now* the leeward side should start hauling in as soon as there is slack in the line, and pull as much sheet as possible with each hand while the sail is flapping. On a thirty-footer, the crew should be able to get most of the sheet home before the sail fills.

The crew member now on the windward side should step across the boat, insert the winch handle, and wind it until the sail is fully home. The tailer, meanwhile, should be watching the position of the sail relative to the spreader; with an enthusiastic winchman it is easy to poke the spreader through the sail. The trimmer should stop winding when the sail is a few inches from the spreader and, if necessary, trim the sheet in slowly as the boat settles on the new tack.

The person tailing should cleat the sheet off or put it in the self-tailing jaws, and check that the lazy sheet is free. He should flake the sheet down so that it will run freely, put a few turns on the windward winch, and be prepared for another tack—you never know when you may have to make a quick tack: a boat on starboard tack might creep up on you; a fast-moving powerboat could appear under the lee of the genoa. It is always best to be prepared.

One crewman should trim the mainsheet traveler for the new tack. If there are only three people in the cockpit, the mainsail trim will have to wait until someone is free.

Some crews preset the mainsheet traveler before tacking by easing it down and cleating it off. This is an aid to tacking on boats with large mainsails. Most sailors simply adjust the main after tacking. Whichever way you choose, make sure that *both* sides of the traveler tag lines are cleated. Nothing is more frightening halfway through the tack than to hear the mainsheet traveler slide to leeward with a thundering crash.

The way to maximize boat speed through the tack is to wait until the bow starts to swing and then ease the main traveler slightly, dropping the boom to leeward. This will help the helmsman bring the bow up. As the boat passes through the eye of the wind, let the mainsail sag to leeward slightly to match the jib trim. As the jib comes in, trim in the mainsail. By working the mainsail simultaneously with the headsail, you will reach maximum boat speed faster.

45: Single-Handed Tacking

Sailing single-handed is becoming more and more popular. The key to tacking single-handed is being prepared. Autopilots have helped to simplify the problem of bringing the helm around. If you have one, you can simply dial in the new heading and wait for the autopilot to respond. For the sailor without an autopilot, the operation is slightly more difficult.

First, get the helm prepared and make the sheets ready to trim in on the new tack. Set the mainsheet taglines so that the traveler will slide across and be restrained by the tagline. If you are sailing to windward and the traveler is on the weather side, set the traveler car in the middle of the track and cleat off the taglines. Put three turns on the windward primary winch and put the self-locking winch handle in. Remove all but three turns from the leeward primary winch and hold the sheet in one hand. Turn the helm to bring the boat slowly through the wind. Quite often it helps to hold the boat head-to-wind for a moment or two to let you get the sheet off the old winch and start pulling in the sheet on the other winch. Throw off the old sheet, steady the helm, and continue pulling in the sheet.

Somewhere during this time you'll have to pause and set the helm for the new tack. After that, grind in the new sheet, set the traveler taglines, and adjust the helm until the boat has settled down.

46: Spinnakers in General

What kind of spinnaker should you have? More to the point, what type of hoisting or dousing system should you use?

Spinnakers are available in two major styles. One is the racing spinnaker, which needs a pole with a foreguy and topping lift, as well as a halyard and a sheet and guy to control the spinnaker. The other style is the cruising spinnaker, which may or may not be poled out. A cruising spinnaker is really a development of the spinnaker/genoa hybrid, known in the mid-seventies as a genniker. Today, many manufacturers have various trade names for their own style of genniker. Note that if the cruising spinnaker is to be gybed you will need an additional sheet and/or guy, or you will need to run the entire sheet around the front end of the boat and rereeve it on the other gybe.

Dinghies or small boats often have their spinnakers stowed in a sock or turtle, ready for instant use. The guy is run through the end of the pole and the pole is put on the mast. Pulling the halyard up sets the sail and the sheet trims it in. When the spinnaker is to be lowered, you pull on the downhaul line (which is attached to the middle of the sail and runs through the sock) as you release the halyard. When the sail is down, the pole is stowed and the entire unit is ready for use once more.

On larger craft there are several systems to enable you to hoist your spinnaker in a controlled manner. You can stop the sail, or you can use a tube, sometimes called a spinnaker Sally, but also known by many other names, that is pulled down over the sail.

When the spinnaker is hoisted it looks like a long tube a few inches in diameter stretching from the masthead to the deck or to the end of the pole. The Sally is raised by a light line running through a block at the masthead, and the spinnaker is sheeted in.

To take the sail down, the Sally is lowered by pulling on the downhaul. This effectively douses the spinnaker by putting it back inside its tube. When the sail is totally captive, the halyard is lowered and the tube is stowed in a sailbag, ready for use once more.

47: Gybing Without a Spinnaker

It's blowing twenty-five knots, with gusts hitting thirty, and you must be home that evening. Your only consolation is that the course is dead downwind. All afternoon you've been on starboard gybe, rolling and pitching. The motion is predictable, bow down as the yacht slides down the back of a wave, rolling to port as the wave passes under the boat and speed decreases, slowly coming back upright as the boat tries to climb the next wave, rolling briefly to starboard as the waves slide by, and then repeating the sequence. With everything strapped in, the motion is tough on the helmsman but the going is easy on the crew.

Now you have to gybe. If you don't do it right, you can take the rig out of the boat. What's the easiest way? If there are only two people on board, the gybe should be done in two stages: first the mainsail and then the genoa. Three or four people can gybe both sails together, but you might want to hand the main over first simply to lessen the confusion.

Make sure you have at least three turns on the mainsheet winch, and let go the preventer on the main boom. Handing the mainsheet across will be the hardest job. Preset the leeward runner, if you have one, with three turns on the winch. As the moment to gybe approaches, grind the mainsheet in. (If this threatens to broach the boat, haul in the mainsheet quickly, hand it across, and let go quickly. Try to keep the movement smooth and quick.) When the end of the main boom points at the quarter, the helmsman should turn the boat to bring the wind on the other gybe. (Relative to the hands of a clock, this means the helmsman turns the boat from a position where the wind is twenty-five past the hour to where it is twenty-five to the hour—less then a ten degree change in heading.) At the same time, the man on the weather runner should grind the mainsheet in. As soon as the main is across, pay out the sheet fast, until it is out as far as required.

The helmsman should choose the moment to gybe when the boat is just coming off the top of a wave and is about to blast down the back. While this makes the turn quicker, it also completes the gybe when the boat is at its fastest and the wind is least strong.

If the boat has running backstays, it is best if a third person can operate the runners. The idea is to let go the windward runner just before the gybe and get the leeward runner up tight *before the sail is across the centerline of the yacht.* The leeward runner will become the weather runner *after* the gybe. If there are only two crew, it usually helps if the helmsman can let go the leeward runner just before the boom hits it. (If the boom hits the runner, one or the other could snap or cause a broach. The boom will pull the runner forward as it is eased).

Once the mainsail is across, grind in the headsail sheet until the clew is almost across. Remember not to ease the weather sheet too far before taking up on the leeward sheet. If you do, you may end up with the headsail in front of the headstay and in a difficult position to gybe easily.

Before settling down again, make sure the preventer is reattached and that the mainsheet is snugged up. Check to see that the sheets are led cleanly, without too much potential for chafe. Now you can go back to watching the horizon.

48: Gybing a Dinghy

Gybing in a dinghy is usually a much more complicated job than in a larger boat. On a dinghy, only two people have to do the work that five or six might do on a thirty-footer.

The sequence starts when the helmsman says, "We'll gybe in a moment," or words to that effect. This gives the crew time to get ready. As soon as the order "gybe ho!" is given, things happen quickly.

The helmsman must get outboard to counterbalance the crew's weight. He turns the boat slowly at first, and then quickly through the actual gybe. As the boat turns into the gybe, he lets the mainsheet out to maximize boat speed going into the turn, and then, when the boat is dead downwind, or slightly by the lee, he hands the boom across. As the boom comes across, he should shout "duck" or "heads down" to give the crew time to duck under the boom. The helmsman then climbs to the weather side and retrims the mainsail to the optimum angle.

The crewman meanwhile should get the spinnaker ready for the gybe. He comes inboard and slackens the topping lift. He needn't worry about the foreguy. At the gybe command, the crewman unhooks the pole from the guy, and then from the mast, hands it across the boat, and hooks into the new guy (old sheet). He then rehooks the pole back into the mast, shouts "made," and scrambles to windward. As soon as he is on the weather rail, he should trim the spinnaker for the new gybe.

The sheet and guy should be played by the helmsman if he has time, or by the crew, who may have to cleat one or the other off before handing the pole across. A few points to remember. First, keep the pole as horizontal as possible. If the outboard end swings up it will be hard to control. Second, put a little centerboard down before going into the gybe. This will tend to stop the boat from skating around the corner. Third, steer the boat through the gybe. The crew's job is much easier if the spinnaker is full and ahead of the boat during the operation. Finally, practice gybing with your crew until you can do it quickly, with minimum fuss.

49: End-for-End Gybing

Gybing end-for-end is not something to undertake shorthanded in heavy winds. We learned that at the Half-Ton-World Championships in Chicago some years ago. Al Capone's adopted city, on the shores of Lake Michigan, was living up to its nickname of the "windy city" when we decided we'd pick up a few places on boats that were taking their kites down and gybing, then rehoisting the spinnakers. We unhooked the pole from the mast, lost control, and broached several times before completing the gybe. We also went from second to seventh place.

But end-for-end gybing on a boat under thirty feet need not be quite the

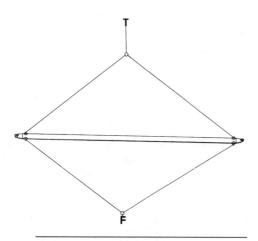

Figure 49-1: A pole used for end-for-end gybing will need a bridle as shown here. T is the topping lift attachment point and F is the foreguy attachment point.

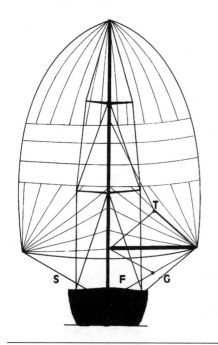

Figure 49-2: The additional lines that you will need to make an end-for-end gybe. T is the topping lift, F is the foreguy, G is the guy or afterguy, S is the spinnaker sheet.

harrowing experience we went through. With proper timing and execution, it can be easy. The first job is to set the boat up for an end-for-end gybe. That means that the pole will require a bridle, as shown in Figure 49-1. The bridle is attached to the foreguy and the topping lift. Generally, a boat making an end-for-end gybe will use a single afterguy/sheet combination, as shown in Figure 49-2. This figure shows the entire boat set up with spinnaker in place.

The actual gybe is quite simple: Figure 49-3 shows the sequence. If the helmsman turns the boat too quickly, the mast man will not have time to get the pole hooked into the new guy or the mast, and will likely lose control of the spinnaker. Thus, the helmsman plays a very large, important role during the end-for-end gybe. The most common reason for screwing it up is that the helmsman doesn't know his part and turns too quickly.

50: The Dip-Pole Gybe

In the days of square riggers, gybing was an all-hands job and completed only with many orders and perfect timing. Even then, an inadvertent mistake could take the masts out of a boat in strong winds. Today, most yachtsmen have only one mast to attend to, and if all else fails, they can take down the spinnaker and re-hoist it on the other tack. But if you are racing, or are interested in improving your sailing skills, you might want to dip-pole-gybe the spinnaker.

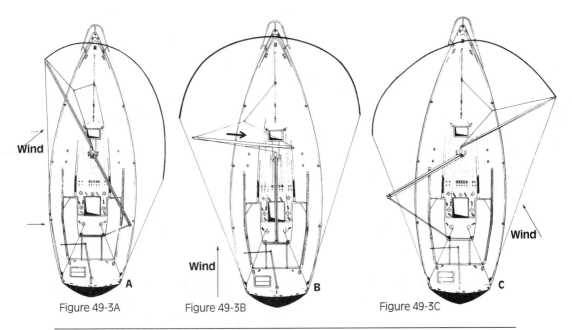

Wind

Figure 49-3A

Wind

Figure 49-3B

Wind

Figure 49-3C

A

B

C

Figure 49-3A, B, C: The end-for-end gybing sequence. With the wind coming from just forward of the port quarter, as shown in A, the helmsman turns the yacht downwind. As the boat is turning downwind, the mainsail trimmer pulls the main in to the centerline. (In lighter winds the mainsail should be let out to maximize speed as the boat is turned downwind, and handed across quickly as the wind crosses the transom.) When the main is on the centerline, the pole is unhooked from the mast and from the port clew of the spinnaker, as shown in Figure B. As soon as the pole is unhooked, the helmsman steers the boat so that it stays under the spinnaker. This step is very important. Do not continue with the gybe, but stay under the spinnaker until the pole is reattached. On the bow, the man handling the pole should clip it into the new sheet before hooking the pole onto the mast. Ease the mainsail out and steer the boat onto the proper course, as shown in Figure C. Trim the pole aft to its correct angle and ease the sheet until the luff is just curling.

Most boats over twenty-eight feet (about 8 meters) overall use the dip-pole method because it is faster and easier than any other way. It requires that the mast, topping lift, and foreguy be marked carefully to ensure that the pole will dip under the headstay without fouling the lifelines. These lines can be marked easily during a session at the dock. All the crew should attend this session and learn the sequence.

Without setting the spinnaker, get the pole ready. Raise the inboard end of the pole so that the outboard end rests on the deck under the headstay. Now raise the outboard end and adjust the inboard height so that the pole clears the headstay and the lifelines. Put a piece of tape or a mark on the mast at the lowest point of the inboard end of the pole. At the same time, mark the topping lift. This will help ensure that during the heat of racing, the pole is preset properly.

Some sailors prefer to use both sheets and guys. Others are happier with just one sheet and one guy. If you use one sheet and one guy, you will have to either add another guy just before the gybe, or you will have to pull the sheet/guy to the bow in order to connect it to the pole as the pole passes under the headstay. This can be difficult in heavier breezes and will also distort the spinnaker, leading to a collapse.

If you are unsure how to make a dip-pole gybe, it is best to practice (without a spinnaker) while the boat is moored at the dock. Start by bringing the pole aft as if the boat is coming into the gybe. Raise the inboard end of the pole to the predetermined height and trip the spinnaker. As soon as the sail is tripped, lower the pole. The man on the bow should pull the foreguy to pull the pole inboard and clip the new guy into the pole. As soon as the guy is locked in, the bowman should shout "made." The pole should then be raised on the topping lift, lowered on the mast until the pole is horizontal, and hauled aft with the afterguy.

That's the practice sequence. Now let's look at the sequence of events during a race. The boat is coming into the mark on starboard gybe with the spinnaker rigged. The bowman pulls the lazy guy forward, taking plenty of slack (additional slack is needed because quite often an enthusiastic tailer will try to pull the new afterguy aft before the set is made). Meanwhile, other crewmen should remove the preventer on the mainsail and raise the inboard end of the spinnaker pole. As the boat squares off to make the gybe, the mainsail is pulled in to the centerline and the spinnaker pole is pulled aft. At the command "trip," the spinnaker is tripped from the pole. The pole is pulled forward and lowered. As it passes under the headstay, the other guy is clipped in. "Made" comes the yell, and the pole and guy are trimmed in. The crew eases the sheet to meet the pole as the latter comes aft. The new spinnaker sheet should be trimmed to suit the position of the sail and the mainsheet should be eased out to its optimum position. Now the boat is on the other gybe. It's that simple.

51: Heavy-Air Twin-Pole Gybing

I once did a long distance race on a fifty-footer where the afterguard in the cockpit could not make up their minds what to do. Should they set a heavier spinnaker or should they gybe? To speed their answer, the crew on the foredeck set the heavier spinnaker on the other gybe, completing what the skipper called the first twin-pole-twin-spinnaker-gybe-change in history. Of course, we couldn't keep the setup flying very long; it would have been illegal. But we got our point across.

While you may not want to change spinnakers at the same time, a twin-pole gybe is fairly easy. It is more work than a dip-pole gybe and requires more time on the foredeck, but I have been told by people who have timed such things that it actually loses less distance than a dip-pole gybe.

Making a twin-pole gybe requires the use of a second spinnaker pole set on the opposite side of the original. Let's say we are going to gybe from port to starboard. Both poles have sheets and guys led to them. Once the starboard pole is raised and positioned at the leeward clew, all that needs to be done is to drop the port pole and gybe the mainsail.

52: Furling and Reefing Sail

In the days of wooden ships and strong men, reefing was accomplished by sending men aloft to tie off each reef in the sail. The men on deck pulled the clews of the sails up to the mast and brailed the sails up to the yards, while men lying over the yards tied in the sail. The whole process was hard work and often done in a howling wind sixty or a hundred feet above the deck.

Fortunately, reefing and sail handling systems on modern sailing yachts are much simpler. On most boats, reefing is accomplished by rolling up the headsail to a predetermined position and putting a reef in the mainsail by pulling the tack and clew downward to the boom.

If you intend to roller-reef your headsail, the sail should be marked for two or three positions. These can easily be set up while the boat is at the dock. First, set the track cars when the sail is full and mark their position on the deck. Next, roll in a set of turns, say three or four. Mark the sail at the tack (and at the head if you send a man aloft) and reset the track car. Now roll in a few more turns and repeat the exercise. This can be done for three or four positions, as shown in Figure 52-1.

The mainsail is a slightly different proposition in that the reefing points are clearly marked and the progression is more orderly. Make sure the reefing lines

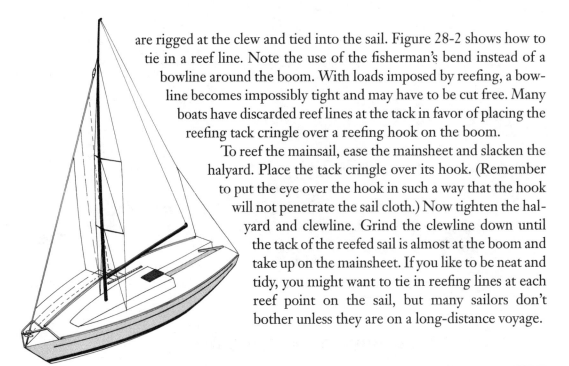

are rigged at the clew and tied into the sail. Figure 28-2 shows how to tie in a reef line. Note the use of the fisherman's bend instead of a bowline around the boom. With loads imposed by reefing, a bowline becomes impossibly tight and may have to be cut free. Many boats have discarded reef lines at the tack in favor of placing the reefing tack cringle over a reefing hook on the boom.

To reef the mainsail, ease the mainsheet and slacken the halyard. Place the tack cringle over its hook. (Remember to put the eye over the hook in such a way that the hook will not penetrate the sail cloth.) Now tighten the halyard and clewline. Grind the clewline down until the tack of the reefed sail is almost at the boom and take up on the mainsheet. If you like to be neat and tidy, you might want to tie in reefing lines at each reef point on the sail, but many sailors don't bother unless they are on a long-distance voyage.

Figure 52-1: Roller-furl the headsail a set number of turns and mark the headsail sheet track. Do this three or four times so that when you are out sailing you will know exactly where to put the sheet lead when the headsail is roller-furled.

53: A Headsail Change

How do you change headsails—The type of sailing you do will usually govern the type of change you make, but taking one sail down before hoisting the second can cost a lot of time, and under mainsail alone the boat may drift into shallow waters. (Most boats make much more leeway under mainsail alone.) Here's a way to change headsails without losing much speed.

You will need to have a double luff groove headstay and twin halyards to do the job properly. Make sure you are on the tack where the halyard in use is on the leeward side—that is, if the jib is hoisted on the port halyard, the boat should be on the starboard tack. Now take the new sail forward, clip the tack in place, and feed the luff into the available groove. Clip on the windward halyard and take up the slack. Take the windward sheet off the old sail and tie it into the tack of the new sail. Hoist the new sail. When it is fully hoisted, tack the boat. The new sail is now to leeward. Drop the old sail (the new sail will keep the old sail onboard) and bag it ready for its next use. Tie the other sheet into the clew of the new sail and you are ready to tack back onto your original course.

54: A Spinnaker Change

Changing the spinnaker usually scares inexperienced sailors. It can be frightening to have two spinnakers flying, neither of which is really under control. But if you take each step carefully and steadily, the job is fairly straightforward. If you are a racing sailor who hasn't yet tried a spinnaker change, practice before you go out onto the racecourse.

You will need a changing shackle or a peeling strop, as shown in Figures 54-1A and B. This is used to clip the tack of the new sail to the pole or to the guy. You will also need an extra sheet; most sailors use the lazy guy temporarily and change to the old sheet as soon as the sail change is made.

A spinnaker change can be made in two ways, either inside or outside the old sail. The easier method is to set the new spinnaker inside and let the old sail peel away from the newly set sail.

To set the new sail, first make sure the halyard is clear of other halyards at the masthead, and that it is led correctly, as shown in Figure 54-2. In most cases, this will mean taking the windward halyard around the headstay before connecting it to the sail. Connect up the new sail in the conventional manner, but take the tack to the changing strop or to the double snap shackle fixed at the pole end. (See Figure 54-1A.) Note that the new spinnaker is carefully stopped to ensure it does not interfere with the already set sail as it is hoisted. Now hoist away!

Once the new spinnaker is at the masthead, break it out by taking up on the sheet. With the new sail set, take the pole forward and release the tack of the old sail, which will peel away from the new sail and can be taken down aft just like a conventional takedown.

If you are in a neck-and-neck race and do not want to lose a moment by taking the pole forward, then a crew member should be

Figure 54-1A: A peeling strop. The spinnaker is set on the strop and the pole brought forward to release the old sail and attach the new sail.

strapped into the bosun's chair and sent out to the pole end. He can then release the sail.

If you are using a peeling strop, you will have to take the pole forward and release the old sail. Then ease the guy to allow the bow man to clip the guy into the tack ring of the new sail before the pole is taken aft. As soon as the old sail is clear, trim the new sail for optimum speed and clean up the deck.

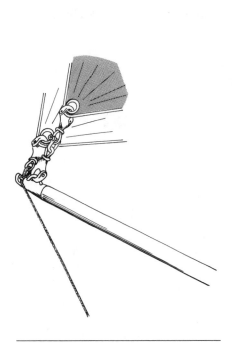

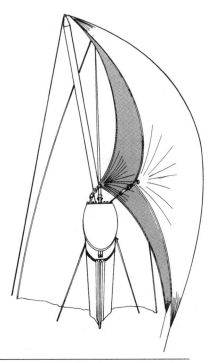

Figure 54-1B: If you do not want to bring the pole forward, a crew member should go to the pole end and attach a changing shackle, as shown in Figure 54-1B. The person on the pole will hook on the new spinnaker and release the old spinnaker.

Figure 54-2: Looking down on the masthead of a boat about to make a change shows the halyards will not cross if the old spinnaker is the outer one. To set up for a second change, the previous halyard can be taken forward under the new spinnaker. If a second change is made and the new spinnaker set under the old one, the halyards will be crossed.

Working the Boat

That the whole is equal to the sum of its parts is nowhere more aptly illustrated than on a boat in which every crew member has an active role in getting to the destination. If the helmsman is not doing his job right, the trip takes much longer. If the navigator messes up, the boat might not get where it is supposed to go at all. Each person has a particular job to do, and all are essential to accomplishing the goal.

In the following section we'll look at some of the techniques that sailors have performed for as long as boats have gone to sea. We'll also discuss some of the shortcuts that the old-time sailors learned before the days of electronic instruments.

55: Helming

Are you a take-charge type—one who comes on watch and can instantly size up the weather, the boat, and the situation before taking the helm? If you are, you may be surprised to learn that you may not be the best helmsman for the job.

The optimum helmsman may be the person who sits on the rail for twenty minutes to get a feel for the boat and the conditions. He may be the one who has tended the mainsheet and helped the helmsman out as gusts loaded up the helm. Here are ten questions to help you rate yourself as a helmsman.

1. Before taking the helm, do you:
a) Check the position of the boats you are racing and take bearings on one or two of the nearest ones?   Yes/No
b) Sit to leeward/windward for a few minutes to get the feel of the sails and the waves?   Yes/No
c) Occasionally check the instruments and the masthead fly or Windex, to get a feel for the wind direction and strength?   Yes/No

You should answer "yes" to all parts of this question. It's important to obtain a complete picture of all the variables before taking the helm. Bearings of other boats allow you to gauge your speed against them. Sitting to leeward and windward and watching the sails, instruments, sea state, and heel angles gives you a few minutes to assimilate all the data and help concentrate, so that when you are steering you do not have to spend the first fifteen minutes building your concentration and letting other boats go by. You should also check with the navigator before taking the helm so that you have a clear picture of what lies ahead.

2. You have the helm and are sailing to windward. Do you:
a) Sit to leeward and concentrate on the headsail telltales?   Yes/No
b) Sit on the centerline and watch the instruments?   Yes/No
c) Sit to windward and watch the sea and the jib telltales?   Yes/No
d) Stand up, concentrate most on the sails, but occasionally glance at the masthead fly, the seas, the weather, and any other boats?   Yes/No

The answers depend upon the conditions. In light air you would probably sit to leeward and watch the telltales, frequently checking the compass and instruments. As the wind builds, the better helmsman will move to the weather side and watch the seas and telltales.

3. **The wind is increasing. You've just taken in a reef and the seas are beginning to pile up. The mark is dead upwind of the boat. Do you:**
   a) Sit to leeward and make small movements of the helm to let the boat's head fall off or luff as the seas hit the bow?   Yes/No
   b) Stand up, watch the seas, and try to edge the bow to windward on the back of the bigger waves, checking the sails all the while?   Yes/No
   c) Squeeze as hard as possible, even if it means losing a fraction of a knot of boatspeed to get to windward?   Yes/No
   d) Steer to the waves and sails, but keep a careful eye on the VMG (speed made good to windward) meter to ensure you are sailing the best combination of speed and wind angle to the mark?   Yes/No

   Going to windward in large seas requires good steering to keep the bow from being knocked off to leeward. The helmsman should be able to see the waves, luff slightly into the bigger ones, and slide down their backs easily without excessive pounding and slamming, which tends to stop forward progress. He should also check the VMG meter occasionally.

4. **How long do you stay at the wheel on a short, inshore race?**
   a) Half hour?
   b) One hour?
   c) Two hours?
   d) Four Hours?
   e) For the duration of the race?

   Various studies have shown that a person's concentration starts to lapse after about a half an hour. The top boats usually change helmsmen every half hour in very light or very heavy winds. In moderate conditions, the helmsman should never steer for more than an hour because they lose concentration and miss the slight windshifts and eddies that enable the best boats to eke out a few extra feet over every section of the course.

5. **How long do you stay at the helm on an overnight race?**
   a) One hour or less on each watch?
   b) Two hours each watch?
   c) The whole watch?
   d) As long as possible?

   A is the correct answer, for the same reasons as above.

6. When sailing on a reach do you:

a) Steer the course regardless of the wind and sea and the amount of helm you use?

b) Ignore any tendency toward weather helm and use up to one complete turn of the wheel to counter it?

c) Watch the compass course, but also watch the seas and puffs of the wind, luffing in the light spots and driving off in the heavy gusts?

d) Ask a crew member to ease the mainsheet in the gusts to enable you to hold course with a minimum of helm?

The best answer is c: You should watch the compass course as well as the puffs and lulls of the wind. The crew should also be tending the sheets, easing them in the puffs when you run off a little and trimming in the lighter patches. The mainsheet trimmer should be ready to let the sheet out if the wheel has more than half a turn on it for more than a few minutes.

7. When sailing in heavy air downwind with the spinnaker up, do you:

a) Steer the course, watching the compass?   Yes/No

b) Watch the seas and the compass and use plenty of helm to keep the boat tracking in a perfectly straight line?   Yes/No

c) Use very little helm and let the bow swing through about 30 degrees either side of the course?   Yes/No

d) Use a combination of b and c as the situation requires?   Yes/No

The answer varies according to conditions. In a confused sea, the helmsman may have to use plenty of helm to keep the boat on course. In most conditions, however, the less the helm is moved the faster the boat will sail. Every movement of the helm absorbs energy that would normally be used to make the boat go faster.

8. Do you know what causes weather or lee helm? Is weather helm caused by:

a) The sails being too full?

b) The mast being too far aft?

c) The keel being in the wrong place?

d) The crew being in the wrong place?

Is lee helm caused by:

a) Light winds?

b) The mainsail being too small?

c) The sails being too flat?

d) The rudder being too far aft?

Answer: Weather helm could be caused by a or b. Usually, the keel's position is determined by the boat's longitudinal center of gravity, and the mast is positioned to reduce or eliminate weather helm in light winds. Putting the crew too far forward can put the bow down and increase weather helm, so the crew would normally come aft in heavy air to minimize helm.

Of the possible causes of lee helm given above, b is the only right answer. Light winds do not cause lee helm, although lee helm is most likely in lighter airs, or when the entire sailplan is too far forward.

9. **You are the watch captain and want to do well on the race. Do you:**

a) Put the nearest crewman on the helm?

b) Try out every crew member before the race to ensure you have a good feel for their potential and put them on the helm as needed?

The correct answer is b. The skipper or watch captain should know who the best helmsman is on each watch and who can steer the best on any point of sail. If not, get to the start early and give everybody a try. You may have a potential expert tucked away.

10. **It's 4 a.m. Your best helmsman has just come on deck and is needed for a critical last leg. Do you:**

a) Put him on the helm immediately?

b) Wait for him to finish his hot chocolate and put him on the helm?

c) Wait for him to get his night vision and then put him on the helm?

The correct answer is c. It takes about twenty minutes to half an hour for people to go from a lighted room into the dark and get their night vision. This is why red lights are used below decks, and why lights should never be pointed aft or used in the cockpit.

56: Helming at Night

I once sailed on a trip in which the on-watch crew fell asleep. The helmsman was awakened by an inadvertent gybe as the boom crashed to the other side. The helmsman had been watching the compass and had become mesmerized by it. Fortunately, nothing was broken, but the bang of the boom woke the entire crew.

Helming at night can be a tricky business, especially if you are not used to it. But the thrill of driving a boat down a tunnel of darkness, listening to the hissing and spitting spume, and seeing the constellations work their way across the heavens is something that every sailor should experience.

The major rule for nighttime sailing is to familiarize yourself with the boat during the day so that you can find what you need in the dark. Make sure you can lay your hands on the jib halyard or the spinnaker foreguy, or any other of the sail control lines. Make sure you know where the compass dimmer switch is, where the engine controls are, and where all the emergency equipment is located. Preparation for helming at night starts as soon as you come on watch. Try to get on deck early so that your eyes can adjust to the darkness. Night vision can often take as long as half an hour to acquire if you have been in a well lit cabin.

But before coming on deck and taking over the helm, check the log to see if the wind speed or direction has varied much over the previous watch. Check the course and dead reckoning position and, if necessary, plot a position (or have the navigator do it) so that you are perfectly sure where you are and where you are going. Then take your hot cocoa and go on deck. Once your night vision is adjusted, check the horizon for other vessels and figure out their relative positions.

Once on the helm, check the relative positions of other vessels again so that if you veer off course, you'll notice a shift in their positions. Check the horizon for stars and pick out one in front of you. Check your compass course to make sure the star really is in front of you and steer for it. Keep checking the compass against the relative position of the star until you have settled in to steering. As soon as you are at ease, check the wind instruments and compass. These should be used as a check only, not as the primary helming guides.

A little understanding of how the wind instruments work will help you understand why you should not use them to steer by. The wind instruments and compass are updated several times a second and then averaged in the instruments' electronic systems before any adjustment is made to the arrow or figures on the dials. This means that the instruments always lag behind the course of the wind or the boat. Consequently, if you watch them you will always be correcting for errors that you created twenty or thirty seconds before. It is like driving a car with a very loose power steering: the car will be wandering and you will be overcorrecting in order to compensate. When you steer by the compass and wind instruments, you always overcompensate as you track the course of the yacht.

Following a star out in front of the yacht is the only way to steer correctly at night. If there are no stars, you should sail by the position of relatively stationary clouds or other landmarks on the horizon, and by your feel of the boat, or seat of the pants sailing, as it was once called.

57: On the Racing Foredeck

The less time the crew spends on the foredeck, the faster a boat will go. Fast, flawless foredeck crew are few and far between; they need experience, strength, speed, agility, confidence, and a thorough knowledge of foredeck procedures.

The foredeck crew's work begins before the race starts. They should lay out the sheets and guys and make sure they are led to the correct winches, or are locked off properly. The foredeck crew makes sure that the right sails for the race are on board, and that they are stowed properly. They also make sure that the spinnakers are flaked or stopped and stowed in the correct bags.

During the race, the foredeck crew will spend a lot of time sitting on the rail. Most of the work is done when sails are changed, or at the turning marks.

Changing Genoas

The decision has been made to change the genoa. As the crew hand the new sail forward, the foredeck man will prepare the halyard and take the sail to the bow, clip on the tack and the sail bag or sausage, the sheets, and the halyard and, as soon as the new sail is feeding properly into the luff groove, he will get ready to pull in the old sail as it comes down. When the sail is down, the crew flakes it, ties it off, and hands it back to be stowed below, ready for use again. As soon as the sail is stowed, the foredeck man should check the halyards and sheets to make sure they are clear for the next change and remove the sail bag.

Setting the Spinnaker

Most foredeck men will spend a while getting ready for a spinnaker hoist, but they shouldn't. With some foresight, everything should be ready to go while the boat is still heading up the first beat. The first step is to run the sheets and guys forward before the race starts, and as soon as the navigator knows on which side the boat will round the first mark. If the mark must be left to port, then the sheet can be clipped onto the first port side stanchion aft of the pulpit and the guy led around the headstay and clipped onto the same stanchion. The halyard can be cleared and made ready, except for bringing it around the back of the genoa.

When the boat gets to within a hundred yards of the turning mark, the foredeck man can dash forward carrying the spinnaker, hook it onto the stanchion base and clip on the sheet and guy, while another crewman brings the halyard around the back of the genoa. The other crewman can hand the halyard to the foredeck man, who clips it on.

At this point, the boat should be very close to the mark and the afterguard can preset the pole by raising it and pulling the guy aft until the spinnaker clew is at the end of the pole. The foredeck man can help by lifting the outboard end of the pole, but he should be careful that the entire spinnaker does not come out of the bag.

When the command comes to hoist, the halyard is hauled up by the mastman and the pole pulled aft to its position. The afterguard should trim the sheet in to break out the stops, and then let the sheet out. As soon as the sail has broken out, the genoa should be dropped. The foredeck man will gather the genoa and flake it, ready for rehoisting. He should then check to see where the genoa sheets are led. If the boat will make several gybes, it is best to relead them so that they are not over the pole.

Changing the Spinnaker

Most spinnaker changes are made by peel changing—that is, raising the new spinnaker either inside or outside of the old spinnaker. The major requirement for a clean peel change is that the halyards run clean. If the halyard for the new sail is twisted under or over the old halyard, it may be impossible to get either halyard down.

The foredeck crew's job is first to make sure the halyards are clean, then to get the new sail ready and clip on the new sheet and peeling strop. Crew may go out to the end of the spinnaker pole and clip the new tack directly to the pole. To do this requires a chair and careful halyard tending. When the new sail is clipped on, it should be hoisted and the previous one taken down. The foredeck man will help to get rid of the sail and then clean up the foredeck.

Gybing the Spinnaker

When making a dip-pole gybe, the foredeck crew operates at the very point of the bow. The job is to clip in the new guy as the spinnaker pole passes under the headstay and through the foretriangle. The mastman will trip the pole off the sheet. The crew in the cockpit will lower the pole and take up on the foreguy.

For an end-for-end gybe, the foredeck man unclips the pole from the spinnaker guy and then from the mast. Next it is handed across the foretriangle, clipped to the sheet that will become the new guy, and hooked into the mast. The rest of the work of gybing is done by the cockpit crew.

Dropping the Spinnaker

For a spinnaker drop, the foredeck man gets the genoa ready to be hoisted by feeding the luff into the groove and clipping on the halyard. When the genoa is fully hoisted, the crew trips the spinnaker from the pole and helps gather the sail if it is taken down on the foredeck. Once the sail is clear, the foredeck man takes the pole down and releads the sheets and guys. Needless to say, crew should work as quickly as possible and get off the foredeck as soon as they can.

58: On the Foredeck at Night

Going on the foredeck at night is always fraught with risk, and many sailors recommend that harnesses should always be worn at night. After many years working the foredeck in many long races, I believe harnesses are essential in rough weather, but in lighter going, a harness gets in the way (I only fell overboard once).

The rule here once again is be prepared. Before dark it pays to check that every halyard is clear and runs freely, and to note where each one is clipped on. A quick look up the mast will usually tell you if anything is twisted. If this is done before darkness falls, you will not need to shine a light up the spar if you decide to change from a jib to a spinnaker at 3 a.m.

The night foredeck man also should know where all the sails are stowed below deck. If a sail change is required, the new sail can be pulled on deck without having to dig through piles of sailbags and waking the offwatch. It also pays to ask the navigator if any major course changes or wind shifts are expected. If you are about to round a racing mark, or change course around a headland, you may be able to prepare the new sail and the needed lines before everyone goes off watch.

When you go forward at night, keep a waterproof flashlight in your pocket so you can check knots, unclip halyards, and sort sails without having to call aft for a light. Also, if the worst should happen and you fall over the side, you will have a light handy to guide the boat back to you.

Another handy item when going forward is a sail tie. Sail ties can be used for anything, tying sails down, as a temporary lashing for the spinnaker pole, as a lashing to keep your hat on, or even for tying the mainsail to the boom. Good foredeck hands often have sail ties stowed by the mast or tied around their waist, ready for instant use.

59: Watch Keeping

On short, overnight races, the entire crew generally stays on the rail all night. Unfortunately, this is not a good practice because it means that the entire crew becomes drowsy between 3 and 4 A.M., and performance suffers. If you really want to win, you can make the largest gains in the early morning hours when the other crews are at their lowest peak of efficiency. The watch rotation system is designed to keep the crew alert and pushing hard all night long, and it is set up around half-hour intervals as follows (for three crew):

Helm - 30 minutes
Windward rail - 30 minutes
Sheet trim - 30 minutes
Windward rail - 30 minutes
Helm - 30 minutes
Windward rail - 30 minutes
Sheet trim - 30 minutes

This leaves 15 minutes at each end of the watch to get acclimated and to wake the other crew members.

The overall watch system can be set up in several ways. The most usual is four hours on and four hours off, with split dog watches to ensure that one crew does not get the midnight-to-four a.m. watch every night. Another option is four-hour watches at night and two six-hour watches during the day. This, too, ensures that the graveyard watch changes every night.

I recently sailed a race to Bermuda, where we worked three-hour watches, changing at 12, 3, 6, and 9 o'clock. At first I thought this system would give too little sleep to the off-watch, but after using it for 24 hours, I liked it. Three hours goes by quickly and the crew stays alert for the full watch. On a four-hour rotation, it always seems as if the last half hour drags. With three-hour watches, the crew was fed on deck at the watch change and managed to get enough sleep, except when an all-hands was called.

Other systems use variations on this theme. One system, used mostly for cruising boats, has six-hour shifts for the night watch to enable the crew to get as much sleep as possible. Another has two eight-hour shifts at night and two four-hour watches during the day.

The system you select should be consistent with your goals. If you are racing, a three-on, three-off (or even shorter) watch system tends to be the most efficient. Cruising sailors have different priorities and would most likely use a variation that gives them a longer time off-watch at night.

Whatever system you select, it is usual, on fully crewed boats, for the cook and the navigator not to take a watch. The cook will often get up at each watch change to ensure the watch going on has a hot drink before going on deck, while the navigator might stay up to hear weather forecasts, take sun sights, or to check the Loran or Satnav reading; or be on deck continuously when making a landfall. On short-handed boats, both the cook and the navigator stand watch, and meals generally are served around the change of watch.

60: Sailing Offshore

When you sail out of sight of land, the crew becomes a microcosm of the world. Each person has his or her own thoughts, ideas, and principles. Each has to work with the other crew members to get the boat safely to its destination. Sometimes the crew is incompatible and friction results. At other times, even though the going is rough, the crew remains friendly.

Part of the secret to remaining compatible is to try out the entire crew before going offshore (sailing beyond the 100 fathom curve, or off soundings). A short afternoon sail can often reveal quite a lot about a particular crewman, and an overnight trip will show you how that sailor is likely to act and react over a longer period. Of course, it has been said that you need at least three days offshore for the politeness to wear off, and only on the fourth day will you begin to really see how crew react to each other. For instance, the crewman may be great at tying knots and setting sails, but the moment he's in his bunk he snores so loudly that the chainplates vibrate. Obviously, unless you are deaf, this is not the crewman to share a small cabin with night after night.

In selecting crew, look for people who know what they are doing on a boat. Some people are so natural on a boat they seem born to it. Others have to work hard at it, but this alone shouldn't be a drawback—it's the people with annoying habits who drive you nuts. The person who cracks his knuckles at inopportune times, or the one who loses it under stress and yells at other people. These are the crewmen who should only be aboard for short trips.

Picking the right crew is only part of the job of sailing offshore. Another part is checking the entire boat carefully. Some boat owners say, "I know the yard did a great job only last week in checking the boat, so I don't need to do anything." The yard workers are not the ones who are sailing offshore. I know of at least three boats that left the yard only to sink halfway to their destinations. In each case, the boatyard made a mistake. At the start of one offshore trip, I went to the masthead to align the wind instruments of a boat that had just come from the yard. On the way down I checked all the masthead fittings and found that the spreader roots were cracked. The mast had just been hauled, and we guessed that the yard had bent the spreaders slightly when lifting the spar out of the boat. Nobody had checked the mast before it was put back.

A good, reliable check should start at the masthead and work slowly through the entire vessel. Below is a checklist to help you organize the task. Go over it before you set sail on a voyage that will take you more than 100 miles offshore.

Spar and Rigging Check

- Make sure the wind instruments are aligned properly at the masthead. Check that the masthead light and navigation lights are working properly and are as watertight as possible.
- Check the halyard sheave blocks for wear, and replace if badly worn. On the way down the mast, check the tube for cracks and dents, especially around rigging attachment points, halyard boxes, and splices or joints.
- Check the halyards for wear and meathooks. Check the halyard snap shackles for wear and alignment. Replace if damaged.

- Check the spreader roots, spreader ends, and fore and aft sides for wear from the halyards. Check also the halyard splices and tails for wear.
- Check all the standing rigging pins and turnbuckles and make sure everything is taped to prevent snagging.
- Check the spinnaker track and cups (if fitted), and make sure everything runs freely. Check also the ends of the reaching strut (jockey pole) to make sure they move freely.
- Look over the boom and make sure all parts of it move freely, especially the outboard end adjustment. Make sure the reefing lines are free to run and their lockoffs (if fitted) work properly. Check, too, the mainsheet and traveler to ensure that everything moves freely and works properly.
- Check the vang and any hydraulic fittings to make sure they have no corrosion and that fluid levels are correct. Make sure there is additional fluid on board.
- Look over the mast boot and spray it with a hose to ensure that there are no leaks.

On Deck
- Remove the barrels from every winch and check for signs of wear and damage. You might want to invest in a repair kit available from the winch maker. The winch may need to be greased. If so, use only the maker's recommended grease. Other greases can react with salt water and clog the gears.
- Check all the anchor gear and other fittings for sharp edges and remove them. Check that the anchor well is properly drained or watertight. Make sure the anchor is secured tightly, and that the windlass (if fitted) is reasonably watertight or well protected. Make sure you have an anchor light.
- Check that all hatches are watertight by spraying water over them. Make sure you have a place to secure halyard tails.
- Check all the sheet tracks and cars for bent pins and freedom of movement. Make sure all fairlead cars can be moved easily and that backup cars are on the track where needed.
- In the cockpit and along the bulwarks, make sure that all the drains work properly and that water drains away quickly.
- Check the steering cable, pedestal, and gears for wear or corrosion. Make sure the emergency tiller can be fitted and used easily.
- Check the gas locker to ensure that the drains are open and that there is no other gear in that locker.
- Get the compasses aligned by a qualified adjuster.
- Make sure the Dorade vents are high enough to prevent green water from going below. In severe storm conditions, the vents need to be at least a foot off the deck.

Lifesaving Gear
- Make sure that the life rings, man-overboard pole, dye marker, drogue, and strobe lights are easily accessible. Check the battery in the strobe light.

- Check that all the harnesses and life jackets are in top-notch condition. Make sure whistles and flashlights are attached to each lifejacket.
- Check the life raft to make sure the inspection sticker is current and that the raft is large enough to carry all the crew. Make sure the raft can be thrown over the side quickly and easily in an emergency.
- Check that the entire crew knows how to switch the VHF to channel 16 and switch the single sideband radio to 2182 or any other emergency channel.
- Check all navigation lights to make sure they are watertight and that there are battery-powered backup lights on board. Also make sure you have spare batteries for all lights.

Below Deck

- Check that each through-hull fitting has a double hose clamp and that a wooden bung is tied near each fitting. Should the fitting break, the bung can be hammered in the hole to stop the water from coming in. Check also that every through-hull fitting is easily accessible and labelled.
- Check the rudder bearings, if possible, for wear and corrosion. Also look over the steering system. Make sure the sheaves are firmly seated and that wire guards are fitted to prevent the steering cables from jumping off the sheaves. Look over the steering cable for signs of wear.
- Make sure all hatches can be dogged tightly, and that those over two square feet in area have storm boards that can easily be fitted.
- Make sure the companionway boards are easily removable and can be fitted in a storm to prevent water from going below.
- Make sure the batteries, stove, fuel tanks, water tanks, and any other large fittings are securely fastened to prevent spillage if the boat rolls upside down.
- Make sure leeboards are fitted in every berth and that there is at least one spare berth.
- There are two schools of thought on floorboards. One says they should be screwed down in case the boat is rolled; the other says that they should be removable in case the hull is punctured. I prefer to have the floorboards held down with a locking mechanism so that they can be removed if desired.
- Make sure that the stove has a remote turn-off valve near the galley and in the propane tank locker.
- Check the keel bolts for signs of corrosion and make sure they are very tight. If the keel bolts are loose, the boat may have a structural problem and should be hauled and carefully looked over by a competent surveyor.

Maintenance and Storage

It has been said that the best sailors are those who are best prepared. Certainly this is true for sailors who sail long distances offshore. If you forget to have the flares checked, and they don't work when you need them, you could put the entire crew at risk. This example illustrates that preparation for sailing is not just a matter of remembering to put certain items on board—it is also making sure that the boat and its equipment are in tip-top condition at all times, easily able to withstand the rigors of a long cruise or an offshore gale.

This section is about maintenance. It looks at what you can do to keep your boat in good repair, both during the sailing season and in the off-season months. It also looks at the preplanning you can do to make your boat and sails operate without breakdowns, the organization of your onboard stowage, and many other factors. Each of these items may seem insignificant on its own, but together they go a long way to making a sailing trip more enjoyable.

Sadly, summer comes to an end and all too soon it is time to get the boat ready to be hauled and stored. While the past season is fresh in your mind, make a list of all the jobs that need to be done. That way, you won't forget them in the depths of winter.

The next job is to get the interior ready. Remove all the sails (this includes sails in sail bags as well as sails stowed on spars), take them home and wash them. Choose a dry sunny day and lay the sails out on the lawn. Wash them with a garden hose and plenty of dishwashing soap. Your goal is to get the salt out of the sail fabric. Once the sails have been washed, they should be dried thoroughly, carefully folded, and stored in a warm, dry place, away from mice or insects. If you don't want to wash the sails yourself, take them to a sailmaker, who probably can store them for the winter as well.

Next, take all food off the boat and scrub the icebox or refrigerator and the lockers. Remember to clean behind the stove and in the corners of lockers. Add a dash of bleach or disinfectant to the washing liquid to reduce the potential for mildew. When you have finished, wedge the locker doors open so that air can freely circulate. This will also help prevent mildew.

Remove all cushions and bedding and give the inside of the boat a good scrub. Again, add a little bleach or disinfectant to the washing liquid and work over the head compartment thoroughly. This is especially important if you have taken showers on board. The grease and gunk that accumulate in the shower sump can create bad odors next year if they dry out over the winter.

Remove all electronics that can be stolen. If you plan to leave electronic gear aboard, take the batteries out and replace them with fresh batteries next season. Some owners even remove the yacht's batteries and charge them at home to make sure they are fully charged next season.

Taking everything off the boat at the end of the season has several advantages. Not only do you prolong the life of your equipment by keeping it warm and dry, but you also remove the junk that collects over a season and slows the boat down.

Now is also the time to get rid of all the water in the water tanks. Pump it overboard and turn off all the plumbing through-hulls. You might also want to pump some fresh water and disinfectant through the head so that the plumbing and sump tanks are reasonably clean.

In the engine compartment, the engine should be run and the salt water cooling system flushed with fresh water. You can wait until the boat is hauled and have the yard do this, or connect a hose to the engine intake line and inject water through the system. The engine oil should also be drained, flushed, and replaced. Remember to drain and flush the engine's fresh water cooling system and hot water tank. Once the boat is hauled, close all the remaining through-hulls so that small animals cannot nest in them.

When the boat is hauled, the mast should be removed. If it is left standing, winter winds can cause the rig to vibrate and ultimately shorten its life. Before the mast is pulled, you might want to mark the turnbuckles so that you know approximately how much to tighten the rigging next year. When the mast is out, it is easy to check it over and to make any adjustments. Check the rig for worn sheaves, bent pins, frayed halyards, and chafed aluminum. Check also for corrosion at the bottom of the mast, and get any problems seen to over the winter. You might even want to tie a messenger on each halyard and pull it out of the mast to wash the salt out of it (to prevent it from stiffening), or install new halyards next season if the old ones are frayed.

Ideally, the deck should be covered for the winter. The simplest method is to lay a tarp over the boat and tie it down, but getting on board requires removing the tarp. A better method is to have a local plumber make up a few arches that fit in the stanchion sockets. Remove the stanchions, insert the arches, and put a boat cover over the boat. This will give you room to move around the boat while keeping the winter snow off the vessel. Remember to tie the cover down tightly.

If you decide not to cover the boat, at least try to cover all the varnish work. If that's impossible, make sure that you have at least six or eight coats of varnish on the brightwork and be prepared to cut it back and apply one or two new topcoats in the spring. If you have a laid teak deck, it should be cleaned, oiled and covered prior to putting the boat away to maintain its appearance. If the deck is non-skid fiberglass, it should be cleaned before putting the winter cover on the boat.

Winches should be covered to prevent corrosion, but if you do not have covers, a light spray of oil will help. Do not use too much oil or it may leach onto the surrounding areas. The compass should be removed and stored in a shaded, dry spot; if the alcohol is heated by the winter sun and then cooled by nighttime frosts, it can create an air bubble in the compass. If you cannot remove the compass, make sure it is covered.

62: Winter Work

If you didn't preplan your winter work and your boat has been sitting in the yard all winter, under cover and ignored, you may have to scramble to get ready for the new season. However, by carefully allocating a certain amount of time over the few weeks before launching date, you can get your boat ready to go. First, you'll have to figure out what needs to be done. If you didn't do it at the end of last season, take a notepad and go through the boat carefully, listing every task. Also list how much time you expect the job to take.

You can make headings for the following categories: sails, the deck, the interior, the underbody, the rig, the rudder, and the trailer. When you have finished listing the work that needs to be done under each category, you will immediately know what state your boat is in. Here's what to look for in each category.

Sails

Lay the sails out on the lawn or in the basement. They should be dry and free of mildew. Check first for worn or ripped stitching. If you have a line of stitching with more than one row missing (usually sails are sewn with three or more rows of stitching at each seam), send the sail to a sailmaker for repair as soon as possible; rates are lowest in winter. Check the corners and make sure the rings aren't distorted. If they are, the sail needs to go to the sailmaker. Check all the hanks and luff ropes. Worn hanks or torn luff ropes will lead to problems later and should be fixed.

Check the mainsail slides and get them fixed if needed. Pull each spinnaker from its bag and check it over carefully. Make sure the masthead swivel is free, that no stitching is frayed, and that the sail has no rips or tears. Repair any small tears with ripstop. You might want to get the spinnaker prepped and ready by carefully flaking it into the bag or even stopping it with rubber bands. If you need additional telltales, now could also be the time to sew them onto the leeches of the mainsail and the spinnaker, and also about nine inches aft of the luff of the genoa.

Deck Gear

Almost every winch will need to be stripped, cleaned, and regreased. Remove the retaining screw or circlip and pull off the drum. On most modern winches, the entire guts can be removed easily by pulling a few pins. Put each part into a plastic or metal bowl. (It pays to keep the pieces of each winch separate or you might find that on reassembly you have created a 90 to 1 ratio rather than the expected 20 to 1.) The old grease, which has probably combined with salt to make a sticky mess, can be removed by soaking the guts in kerosene or another grease remover. Regrease the bearings, spindle, and other moving parts and oil the pawls. If you grease the pawls, you run the risk of having them stick together later in the season, rendering the winch useless. In fact, if your boat is raced regularly you should probably just oil the entire winch, but you will have to reoil several times during the season to ensure maximum efficiency. Oiling has the advantage of allowing the drum to turn faster and run freer, but it requires more maintenance. Finally, carefully reassemble the winch.

Remove all the blocks and degrease those that need it, then regrease or oil them. Do not add grease or oil to blocks with Teflon or other high-tech bearings without checking with your supplier. Check that all the winch handles and other equipment stored in your basement is in tip-top shape. If you haven't already done so, soak all lines in fresh water with a dash of dishwashing liquid. This will soften them and make them easier to handle.

The Spar

While you may not be able to get the mast into your basement, you should spend some time going over it carefully. Start at the bottom. Does it show any signs of corrosion? If so, paint the area with a moisture-resistant paint (not copper-based). You should also pull each halyard (tie a messenger to the end before pulling it out of the mast), then wash it in fresh water, check the splice for signs of wear, and dry and oil the shackle.

Check the spreader end fittings, and make sure they are well padded. Look for cracks in the inboard ends, especially where the spreader pins or fixes to the mast. Check each entry and exit box on the mast and make sure that stainless steel chafe strips are installed wherever chafe may occur between wire halyards and aluminum masts, usually at the top and bottom of the exit box. At the masthead, check the sheave boxes. Look for worn pins and sheaves, missing bearings, and unexpected chafe. Replace or repair any broken or worn fittings. A damaged sheave can chew through a halyard in a few hours. While you are looking at the masthead, check the alignment of the Windex or wind instruments. It should be on center. Spray CRC or some other dryer into the instrument coupling to ensure a good, season-long connection.

63: Getting Ready for Spring

The Underbody

You'll need to scrape all those barnacles off and sand the hull thoroughly if you intend to race well. Start by scraping as much of the old antifouling off the hull as you can, then sand it smooth. (Use one of several commercially available paint strippers; paint chips are now recognized as a significant hazard to the environment.) You may have to putty various areas to ensure total smoothness and to fill the spots where you dinged the dock or the rocks. Take your time and get it right.

Make sure the keel and rudder are faired and smoothed. When sanding the bottom, work aft from the bow. It is especially important that the first third of the boat be smooth, because this is the area in which laminar flow takes place. The longer laminar flow stays attached to the hull, the lower the drag will be and the faster you will sail in lighter going. The same applies to the keel and rudder: laminar flow takes place in the first third of the appendage and that should be the smoothest. Any bumps or bubbles in the forward part of the boat will break up the flow and immediately increase the drag. (When you are sailing, the same rule applies. A sudden movement or bump on deck in very light winds destroys laminar flow and slows the boat.)

If you like your boat to look neat, this is also the time to polish and wax the topsides. You might also want to touch up the boot top and cove stripe if they are at all damaged.

On Deck

If there are any areas that leaked last year, now is the time to remove the fitting, apply a heavy layer of silicone caulking, and replace the fitting. Check also that cleats are smooth in all directions, that lockoffs work easily, and that rope tail bags and winch handle pouches are in place.

Wait for a day with temperatures over 50°F before you even think about varnishing. Always varnish in the middle of the day, when there is no chance that dew or moisture will turn the varnish muddy. Teak oil can be applied to unvarnished areas at the same time of day to make the cockpit soles and seats look clean and attractive.

Remember to check your bow roller and anchor-handling system. Look for areas of potential chafe. It might also be time to make up a new anchor pendant and whip. Check that the end fitting on your spinnaker pole works properly and that all the hatches seal properly and have fly screens. An ounce of prevention now can save you hours of cursing later.

Inside the Hull

It might also be time to inventory everything you put aboard the boat. This serves several purposes. First, should the boat sink, you will have an inventory for insurance purposes. Second, an inventory will allow you to see how much unnecessary junk you take aboard. Third, it might help you sail leaner and faster, if you race regularly.

64: The Maintenance Log

If you rely on memory to get broken gear repaired, you need to start a maintenance log. Like the little sticker the garage puts on your car to tell you when the engine oil was last changed, the maintenance log serves as a reminder to get things done. Kept properly, it also will tell you when overhauls are due, when the item was last repaired, and when the warranty runs out on a piece of gear.

To set up a perfect maintenance log—that is, a log of all breakdowns or gear failures during the season—make up a page with six columns on it. Let's say a winch broke. In column one, note which winch it was. In column two, enter the date the problem developed. Write the cause of the problem in column three (for example, the winch pawls clogged up due to use of the wrong grease when the winch was lubricated during preseason fitting out). In column four, record the action taken; for example, the winch was stripped, cleaned in kerosene, and regreased using Lewmarlube for winches. Column five will show the date the work was done. Column six is for remarks, such as a note to check any other winches that were relubricated during spring fitting out—they too might be coated with the wrong grease.

About one third of the way through the logbook, make a haul-out checklist to show exactly what is to be done when the boat is hauled at the end of the season. For instance, this list will remind the owner or yard to drain the hot water heater and flush the engine water system. At that time, the filters should be replaced and the engine unit lubricated. The grease seal on the shaft should be checked for wear and replaced over the winter if necessary. This log should also list any additional work that needs to be done over the winter.

In the middle of the logbook, make the spring checklist with a complete record of all the work done on the boat during the spring fitting out period. It should list everything from the type of paint used on the bottom to the type of grease used in the winches.

At the back of the logbook, list all the items of equipment on board the boat. Next to each item, note its serial number, cost, warranty period, where it was purchased, and any modifications that were made in order to get the gear to work. You might also want to make a copy of this list for your insurance company.

The maintenance log, then, is a compendium of data on every piece of gear on the boat. It can be used to keep track of repairs, but it will also serve as a complete record of the boat's expenses, plus a valuable sales tool when you decide to sell the boat. The new buyer will immediately be able to see how much has been done and how much it cost.

65: Where Is It Stowed?

Do you have a storage plan for your boat? If you don't know what a storage plan is, you may be a sailor who crawls around below decks looking for a piece of equipment for several hours while everyone else is enjoying the sail.

Simply put, a storage plan tells you where everything is stowed, from the food in the galley to the sails in the forepeak. The simplest plan is a sketch of the boat, with a list on each locker of the gear stored inside. A copy of the designer's plan view of the boat (see Figure 65-1), for example, can be laminated or covered by a sheet of clear plastic so that you can write on it with a grease pencil.

Another method of keeping a storage plan is to make a list of all the essential items on board and write down where each one is stowed. The following

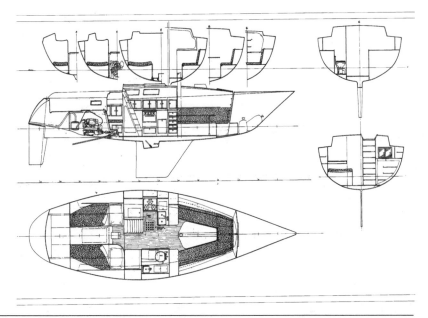

Figure 65-1: Use a drawing of the interior of your boat to mark where every item is stowed. This drawing will be invaluable if you go on a long cruise.

list is intended to be as broad as possible and can be easily adapted to suit your boat. Note that some electronic navigation programs such as the Cap'n, from Nautical Technologies Ltd., in Bangor, Maine, allow you to make a list on your computer.

Item	Where Stowed
Batteries (spares)	
Blocks (spares)	
Boat keys	
Bosun's bag	
Bosun's chair	
Bulbs (spares)	
Burgees	
Dock lines	

Item	Where Stowed
Electronics (spare parts)	
Emergency tiller	
Engine (spare parts)	
Engine oil	
Fender board	
Fenders	
Fire extinguisher	
First aid kit	
Flags	
Flares	
Flashlights	
Fog horn	
Fog horn (extra gas canisters)	
Harnesses	
Hose clamps	
Inflatable	
Inflatable repair kit	
Inflatable bellows/pump	
Leadline	
Life jackets	
Life raft	
Loud hailer	
Pump (spares)	
Radar reflector	
Reefing lines and handles	
Rubber bands (for stopping spinnaker)	
Shackles (spares)	
Ship's papers	
Stopwatch	
Stove (spare parts)	
Toolbox	
Winch handles	
Winch (spares)	
Wire cutters	

PART TWO

PERFORMANCE SAILING

Performance sailing runs the gamut from cruising at a fast pace to racing in the America's Cup. A cruising sailor might opt to get the best performance out of his boat, or to get to port before a storm hits. A racing sailor sacrifices everything to get the last hundredth of a knot out of the boat. Both of these types of sailors might experiment to find the best mast trims, sail shapes, and other variables that give them the best boat speed.

In this section we'll look at the many factors that help increase speed. If you are a sailor who loves to race well and to come out on top, the first step is to get your boat in absolute tip-top shape. Then you will have to make sure that your sails are perfectly trimmed, and follow that with finding a top-notch crew to sail with. Finally, you'll have to make a perfect start and sail the race with flawless performance from your crew. Only with all these variables working in your favor are you likely to end up in the silver.

In Part 2 we will look at the many steps involved in winning that big race, starting with getting the boat ready. Then we'll discuss how you can plan tactics and use some advanced techniques to get the best out of your boat.

Tuning a Boat

Whether it involves getting the keel perfectly faired, oiling the winches so that they work perfectly, or tuning the mast to suit the newest sail shapes, getting a boat in good racing trim takes a lot of preparation and hard work. Not only do you have to figure out what makes your boat go fast, but if you are in a one-design class, you'll also need to find out what the winners are doing to win so that you can adapt their tuning methods to suit your own boat's weight, trim, and sails. It helps to have a friend with a similar boat to tune against; you can optimize sails and rigs by racing one another.

But if you're on your own, you'll have to try out various techniques and see which ones work best for you, or use a computer to analyze the information on every technique you try in order to find the optimum speed for your boat. If you do not have a computer, keep a log of everything you attempted, with comments on the resulting improvement or decrease in boat speed. In the following pages, we'll suggest several methods of optimizing performance, many of which will work on most boats. But because boats are so idiosyncratic, you may have to combine techniques and experiments to see what works best for you.

Keels and rudders are generally looked upon as lifting surfaces, just like the wings of airplanes. Consequently, much of their terminology comes from the aeronautical field. *Lift* is generated when the keel moves at an *angle of incidence* to the water flow. In nautical terms, this means that the boat is making a certain amount of *leeway* (angle of incidence) to its *heading* (direction of water or airflow), which gives lift at right angles to the keel centerline. The amount of lift generated depends upon the sectional shape of the keel. Unfortunately, increasing lift often comes at the expense of increasing drag. To determine how much lift-to-drag a keel generates, designers talk about *lift/drag ratios*—that is, the amount of lift divided by the amount of drag. Remember that if both lift and drag go up, the boat will go slower because the driving force of the sails remains the same.

The keel itself has part names just like the wing of an airplane. As Figure 66-1 shows, the area from the top to the bottom of the keel (Sp) is known as the *span;* the area from front to back is called the *chord.* If the chord is measured at the hull it is known as the *root chord* (Cr). If measured at the bottom of the keel it is known as the *tip chord* (Ct), and if measured in the middle it is known as the *mid-chord* (Cm). The angle that the leading edge makes with the vertical is known as the *sweepback angle* (S). Because the leading edge sweepback angle can vary, the point at which the sweepback angle is measured is taken as 25 percent of the chord length. If wings or winglets are fitted to the keel, the winglets use the same terminology.

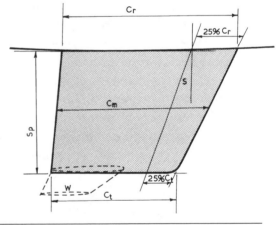

Figure 66-1: Keel terminology. Span is the vertical dimension of the keel, and in the diagram Sp is the span of the keel. The chord is the fore and aft dimension of the keel; Cr is the root chord, Cm is the mid-chord, and Ct is the tip chord. Keels are rarely vertical, but have a sweepback angle. Here, S is the sweepback angle. If the keel has a forward sloping leading edge, the sweepback angle is said to be **negative.** Sweepback is taken at 25 percent of chord length. If the keel has a wing or winglet, shown as W, the span, chord, and sweepback terms apply to them as well.

The sectional shape of the keel is determined by the designer. In the days before computers, most designers used the NACA (National Advisory Committee for Aeronautics) section from a book called *Theory of Wing Sections* by Abbot and Doenhoff (Dover Publications, New York, 1959). This book provides lift coefficients and other keel characteristics. Today, these statistics are available on computer software programs. The most popular programs for keel section statistics and lift and drag information are produced by Dave Vacanti. Programs are KLIFDR (Keel Lift and Drag), FOIL v.3.0 (Aerofoil Shapes), LOFT v.3.1 (Keel and Rudder Design), and WINGS (3d Design Tool), obtainable from Vacanti Yacht Design Software, Renton, Washington. Many yacht designers use these programs.

When a keel is moving through the water, it generates not only lift but also drag, or resistance to forward motion—frictional drag is caused by the rough surface of the keel and directly proportional to the wetted surface; form drag is caused by the shape of the keel. Form drag and frictional drag make up the profile drag of the keel. Another component of resistance is induced drag, caused by aspect ratio, taper ratio, spanwise lift distribution, and vortex drag.

When aeronautical engineer Leonard Green and I were testing a suite of new keels for the 12-meter *Courageous* in the flume tank, we could clearly see the vortices spinning off the ends of the winglets. It was interesting to note that sheet vortices spun off the trailing edge of the keel without winglets, but when winglets were fitted, the vortices were concentrated at the ends of the winglets and reduced the drag.

Like fighter planes with wingtip tanks, some keels sport bulbs at their ends. The bulb is not there for aerodynamic reasons; in fact, many analyses show that it actually increases drag. A bulb keel increases the stability of the yacht, and this increase in stability is often enough to overcome the increased drag of the bulb.

67: Fairing the Keel

How smooth is your keel? Is it full of hollows and bumps, or haven't you looked at it for a couple of years? A smooth, fair keel gives much more lift than a bumpy one, especially in light airs. A discontinuity near the leading edge can stimulate a turbulent flow over the entire keel. This is because, in lighter going, turbulent flow has a much higher resistance than laminar flow, but to get laminar flow the keel must be perfectly smooth and level. Here's how to make yours the envy of the fleet.

Check the keel over carefully. Place a straight edge along the span and check for hollows or bumps. Figure 67-1 shows how a straight edge is laid along the keel.

After checking the keel in the spanwise direction with a straight edge, make a template of the keel sections. You may have to get the information on the keel section from your boat's designer. Only with a correct template can you achieve the designed lift/drag curve for that keel. Figure 67-2 shows what the

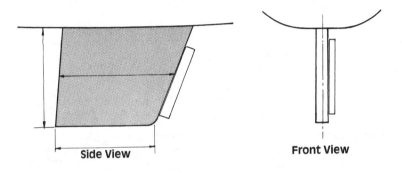

Side View   Front View

Figure 67-1: Lay a straight edge along the keel to show any humps or hollows. Slide the straight edge around the keel and mark the bumps. Sand them off and then fill the hollows with a marine grade filler.

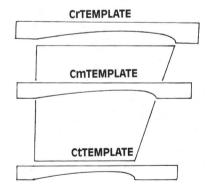

Figure 67-2: Using the sectional chord shapes from your designer, you can make a template and fair the keel fore and aft.

Figure 67-3: Use a long board to fair the keel. The board should be fitted with wet and dry emery or sandpaper for best results and should be flexible.

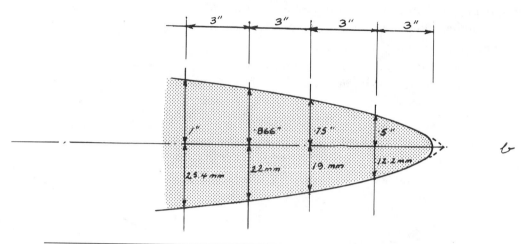

Figure 67-4: To make sure the leading edge of your keel is perfectly faired, you will need to make a leading edge template. Get the information from your designer and lay it out as shown here.

template should look like. Check the keel in the chord direction with the template, and again, mark any hollows or bumps.

Now that you know where all the bumps and hollows are, it's time to get rid of them. Most of the bumps can be sanded off, but you will have to fill the hollows. If you have many hollows, it may be easier to sand the bumps off than to fill all the hollows. Use a long board, as shown in Figure 67-3, to sand the keel, and fill the hollows with either WEST epoxy with microballoons or a commercial filler specified for use underwater. Build up the hollows in thin layers,

Figure 67-5: The shape of the keel's trailing edge is also of critical importance. A shows the best fairing; however, it is difficult to fair the trailing edge into a fine feather. B shows how *not* to do it. The trailing edge is rounded slightly and can create turbulence. C shows how I prefer to see it done, with a 1/4" (6mm) flat on the trailing edge. In D the trailing edge is shown as it typically comes, rounded, from the keel manufacturer. This can create a small amount of turbulence.

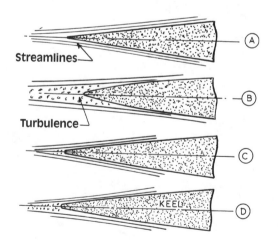

waiting until each layer is dry before applying the next. Lightly sand between layers and check with the straight edge to make sure you are not building larger bumps. Use the template to check along the chord of the keel. Eventually, you'll end up with a reasonably smooth keel.

Now comes the overall sanding. With your sanding board, work at getting the keel smooth both vertically and horizontally. Check frequently with your templates and straight edge to ensure that you are not grinding other hollows into the keel.

Once the sides of the keel are in good shape, the leading edge and trailing edge will need attention. For the leading edge fairing, you will have to make another template. A typical one is shown in Figure 67-4. This too should be obtained from the designer. Proceed in a similar manner to the work undertaken on the sides. Use the straight edge and template frequently to ensure you have a nice fair leading edge.

The trailing edge presents a slightly different problem. Ideally, it should be knife sharp, but that is virtually impossible when a filler or lead has to be shaped. I prefer the trailing edge to be flat and about ⅛" to ¼" wide. This has a similar effect to a sharp trailing edge, but it is easier to produce. Figure 67-5 shows different trailing edge shapes. Note that the leading edge fairing changes at the keel bottom. In other words the parabolic leading edge fairs smoothly into a flat keel bottom. Most designers use a flat bottom surface on their keels to maximize lift. If your keel has a flat bottom surface, make the side/bottom corner sharp.

Next, you'll need to check the hull/keel joint to make sure it is fair. Some designers reserve a small radius at the fillet, while others prefer to make the angle sharp; you should check to find out which is preferred on your boat. If a small radius is required, you can make another template that can be drawn over the fillet to fair it perfectly. Having done that, your keel should be close to perfect. Now it is time to paint the keel with either antifouling or racing bottom paint. Finally, use the finest sandpaper (400 grit) to smooth the entire keel. Work in a chordwise direction to ensure that the keel is smooth in the direction of the waterflow. After all your hard work, you do not want to create unfair sections across the waterflow that might stimulate turbulence.

The same steps can be taken to fair the rudder blade and the bottom of the yacht. This will make the vessel's bottom as smooth as possible and increase boat speed in lighter winds. As the wind comes up, wave-making drag increases and other techniques are required to keep speed high.

Who set up your mast, you or the boatyard? If the yard did the job, it may not be the best it can be. If the mast is not perfectly straight, it can move out of column and collapse. You might want to tune it yourself and see if it can improve your performance.

Before tuning the mast, it helps to understand the terminology used when discussing spars and rigging. Rather than talk about an aft lower shroud or upper shroud, riggers and designers refer to the shrouds by letters and numbers. These are shown in Figure 68-1.

First, check the mast for transverse tune, beginning with a look at the mast wedges. Some racing sailors prefer to have the mast wedges fore and aft of the mast, while others like them on either side. Placing them fore and aft, as shown in Figure 68-2A, is the traditional position: it holds the mast firmly but allows it to move slightly in a transverse direction. My preference is to wedge the mast transversely and allow it to move fore and aft as the mast is bent. Figure 68-2B shows the position of transverse mast wedges. For cruising sailors a relatively new product called Spartite fills the gap between the mast and the partners. To use it, first push a foam wedge up from underneath into the gap between the mast and the partners. Then pour a two-part polymer into the space and leave for 48 hours to set. To remove Spartite at the end of the season, the mast should be lightly greased before installation. Spartite cannot

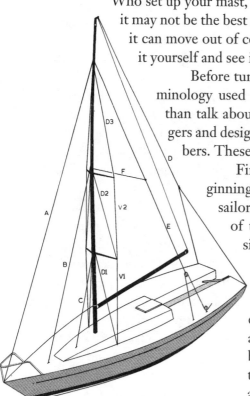

Figure 68-1: Rig terminology. The fore-and-aft shrouds are named as follows: A is the headstay, B is the midstay, C is the babystay, D is the backstay (in this case it is a split backstay), E is the running backstay or runner, and F is the checkstay. The transverse shrouds are D1s, lower diagonals; V1s, lower vertical shrouds; D2s, mid-panel diagonals; V2s, mid-panel verticals; and D3s, upper diagonals.

fall out and can be reused from year to year.

Once the mast is wedged, look up the mainsail track on the back side of the mast. Is it straight? If it is, the next step is to make sure the masthead is in the middle of the boat. Take the main halyard (check to make sure it is on the centerline of the mast) and measure to the rail or chain-plates on either side of the boat. The measurement on both sides should match. If there is a difference in length between one side and the other, the mast-head might not be over the centerline of the yacht, and the boat may sail better on one tack than on the other. If there is no difference in measurement, the masthead is on centerline. Now recheck to ensure that the mast is straight and in the middle of the boat at the partners.

If the mast is not straight and the masthead is on the centerline, you will need to take out the bend in the rig. Figure 68-3 shows how that situation may arise. The port D2 could be too tight, causing the mast to bend. To take out the bend, ease the port D2 and tighten the starboard D2. You will probably have to adjust the V1/D1s on both sides as well.

If the mast has multiple spreaders, you should work from the bottom to the top (start with the D1s, V1s and then adjust the D2s, V2s before tensioning the D3s, V3s). Make sure that each diagonal and vertical shroud is tight and that the mast is straight at each stage. After all the shrouds have been adjusted, sight up the mainsail track to make sure the mast is perfectly straight.

Now it's time to go sailing. Pick a day when the breeze is blowing about ten to fifteen knots, and if you can find the right spot, pick a place where the ocean is fairly flat, such as the lee of a low island. Come onto port tack and check to see if the mast stays straight. Most likely the mast will distort slightly and need retuning. Make a note of the way the mast bends, tack over to starboard, and tighten the leeward shrouds. You should also check how straight the mast is while the boat is on starboard tack. Tack back onto port and adjust the leeward shroud to straighten the rig when on starboard tack.

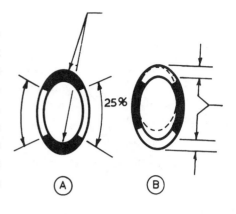

Figure 68-2: Mast wedges placed fore and aft are in the traditional position (A). A better position is to place them transversely (B) and allow the mast to bend slightly in a fore-and-aft direction at the partners.

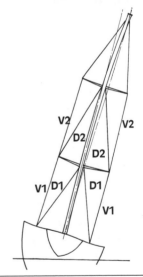

Figure 68-3: If the mast is set up with some bend in it, you will have to adjust the shrouds to eliminate the bend. Here the port D1, V1, and D2 will need to be eased and the shrouds on the opposite side tensioned (refer to Fig. 68-1). After adjustments, the masthead should be checked to make sure it is in the center of the boat.

Check the rig again. You'll probably have to tack several times before the rig is set up perfectly. At this point, on either tack, the leeward shrouds should be tight but not twanging—snug might be a better term. They definitely should not be flopping around. Make sure the mast is perfectly straight on both tacks after any adjustments have been made.

When you are happy with the transverse trim, remember to put cotter pins in all shroud endings and tape them so that they will not rip sails or hands. That's all you need to do to get your mast set up transversely.

69: Longitudinal Mast Tuning

There are so many variations on the optimum longitudinal mast trim that we can only look at basics to help you decide how to make the mast work best for your boat. Fore-and-aft tune should be thought of in three separate contexts:

1. Eliminating or reducing weather helm
2. Making the mast suit your mainsail
3. Setting up for mast bend under sail (see page 135, no. 71, for further details on this step)

To set up for eliminating or reducing weather helm, first determine if, and to what extent, you have this problem. If your boat keeps coming up into the wind at wind speeds of 12 to 15 knots or less, you have weather helm.

Weather helm often can be eliminated by pushing the mast to the forward end of the mast step and all the way forward at the partners. This has the effect of moving the entire sailplan forward. If moving the mast does not work, you may need to reduce the mainsail area by reducing the foot length or roach of the sail. Conversely, lee helm can be eliminated or reduced by bringing the mast as far aft as possible, or by increasing mainsail area.

If you have pushed the sailplan forward to correct weather helm, the mast should be set up straight in the boat. Check the vertical angle by hoisting a plumb line to the masthead and marking its position on the boom. This is best done in the calm of the morning or late evening. Note that the boat should be in sailing trim—that is, with crew or equivalent weight in the crew positions. If the mast is not vertical, you can move the masthead forward by tightening the forestay and easing off on the backstay. The opposite sequence will move the masthead aft. Note also that this operation is done before any hydraulics are applied. Now check that the spar is straight. If not, make adjustments at the mast step, the partners, or at the masthead.

To make the mast suit your mainsail, go sailing with the mast vertical and straight in a fairly light breeze and check the sails. Is the leech of the mainsail tight? If it is, you might want to bend the mast and pull the masthead aft slightly. If the leech is tight in light winds, tighten the backstay and put a little prebend in the mast. This opens the leech of the sail and lets the telltales stream out better. As the wind increases, mast bend can be increased by using a hydraulic backstay. This induces more bend in the mast and tightens the headstay. A tight headstay helps the boat point better.

If the masthead is as far aft as possible and you still have lee helm, rake the mast aft. This will bring the center of effort of the mainsail aft and help load the helm in a breeze. Figure 69-1 shows the difference between bending and raking the mast.

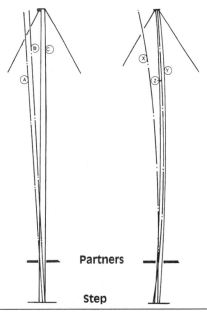

Figure 69-1: This figure shows the difference between raking and bending the mast. In the drawing on the left, the mast is raked aft. In other words, it stays straight and leans aft (A). B shows rake if the mast foot is moved forward. C shows the mast vertical. In the drawing at right, the mast is bent. It does not move at the partners, and the masthead ends up in the same position as the raked mast. If the mast foot is kicked aft bend is induced lower down on the spar (Z). Y shows the mast with some prebend. Raking the mast aft reduces lee helm, while bending the mast aft opens the leech of the mainsail and tensions the headstay.

Weather helm can be eased by raking the mast slightly forward and bending the top aft, although this seems to make the boat slower. This trick is especially helpful if the mainsail is old and full. It is accomplished by kicking the mast heel aft slightly—about a half inch is often all that is needed for a thirty-footer. The top of the mast is bent aft by tightening the backstay. The overall effect is to flatten the middle part of the sail and open the leech. Note that your mainsail wears out with time, and the fore-and-aft mast tune will vary slightly every year. Every season the mast should be bent a little more to eliminate the increasing fullness of your mainsail.

70: Mast Controls

Masts can be moved at the foot, the partners, or the masthead. Although racing rules might permit moving the mast at the foot, this takes a lot of power—on larger boats it is done with hydraulics—so it is not practical for the average cruiser. Moving the mast at the partners is also a job for hydraulics, and although it is an easier task, few racing rules allow it. The majority of the mast's movement must come from above-deck controls. The babystay, midstay, running backstays, and permanent backstay all control the fore-and-aft movement of the mast. The mainsail and foresail affect the mast shape in a more uncontrolled way.

Because of the load exerted on the shrouds and the potential for catastrophic failure, transverse movement of the mast is rarely attempted. When it is done, it is accomplished by hydraulics. For instance, I remember racing against a Chance-designed ketch some years ago where the mizzen could be hydraulically canted to windward to minimize the influence of the mainsail.

Optimum Positions

	Action	Secondary effect	Secondary effect remedies
Tensioned headstay	Tighten backstay	Bends mast	
		Tightens headsail luff	Ease headsail halyard
		Opens mainsail leech	Tighten mainsheet
		Tightens mainsail luff	Ease main halyard
Flattened mainsail	Tension babystay	Bends mast	
		Opens mainsail leech	Tighten mainsheet
		Tightens halyards	Ease halyards
Increased weather helm	Rake mast aft	Lowers boom end	Tighten main sheet
		Lowers headsail tack	Move sheet lead forward
Increased lee helm	Rake mast forward	Raises boom	Ease main sheet
		Raises headsail tack	Move sheet lead aft

When sailing upwind, a tight headstay is of primary importance. Tightening the headstay by tensioning the backstay pulls the top of the mast aft and may cause the mainsail leech to open up, so the mainsheet may also have to be tensioned. The top of the headsail will be pulled aft, and quite possibly, the headsail will be tensioned along the luff, which requires an easing of the headsail halyard. Tightening the headstay, then, means more than just cranking up on the hydraulics; it also means knowing how this adjustment will affect the other parts of the sailplan.

The preceeding table shows what controls to employ in order to tension certain parts of the rig. The third column shows other parts of the rig or sails affected by these control changes, and the fourth column shows how to reduce the effects.

71: Recording Sail Data

For boats with adjustable rigging, varying the mast shape under sail can give you extra speed. The most well known variable is to let the backstay off as soon as you round the weather mark in a race. This moves the masthead forward and lets the spinnaker hang better. Going to windward in light winds, a little backstay tension will bend the top of the mast aft and open the leech of the mainsail, giving better boat speed.

As the wind increases, the backstay/headstay should be tightened. You will need to tighten the vang or mainsheet as well to prevent the mainsail leach from falling off to leeward. This will tend to develop fullness in the middle of the mainsail. Tightening the outhaul will flatten the lower third, and taking up on the babystay will flatten the middle third. Flattening the mainsail will enable the boat to stand up better and go faster.

Make each change carefully and note its effects. Write the changes in a notebook, together with wind speed and any boat speed differences you observe. This way, you will know how to repeat every operation. As wind speed increases, put in the flattening reef. This tensions the leech and foot of the mainsail and generally flattens it. You may also need to take up on the Cunningham line to pull the draft forward again.

While all these adjustments are taking place on the mainsail, the jib will also need work. It should be set up according to the prevailing conditions. Flat water means a slack headstay; an eased halyard, with the genoa cars forward to get a well-rounded foot; and a fairly tight leech to get lots of power out of the genoa. As the wind increases, the headstay should be tightened when the backstay is adjusted to suit the mainsail, and the halyard should be tensioned to remove any wrinkles. The car should be moved aft slightly to remove foot-round and to open up the leech slightly as the sail begins to flatten. Adjust sheet tension to suit the sail shape.

As the wind increases still further, tighten the halyard even more (you may have to use some Cunningham tension if the halyard is two-blocked). Move the car a notch aft and tension the sheet until the sail is just a few inches from the spreader ends (or in the best position for your boat). The sail should be watched constantly to ensure that the spreader ends do not poke through it in the lulls.

More wind means either reefing the mainsail or changing jibs. This call should be made by the helmsman. If the helmsman has too much helm, the choice may be to reef the main first. If the helm is good (about 3 to 4 degrees of rudder angle is best to get maximum lift from the rudder blade) but the boat is heeling too much, the jib should be changed first.

If the wind continues to increase, your options are limited. You can either keep changing jibs and reefing until you are down to the storm sails, or you can go home and wait out the storm.

72: A Sail Tune-up

Take a look at your sails. Do the corners show signs of delamination, stretched stitches, or deformed metal rings? If you see any of these symptoms, your sails are reaching the end of their useful life.

Many modern materials have a short life on the racecourse. To win races, your sails need to be in perfect shape. For instance, many America's Cup campaigns have found that Kevlar/Mylar sails last about 80 to 90 hours on the race course before causing significant speed deterioration. In long-distance ocean racing, a sail might see that much wear in one race alone. For the sailor who races in local waters, sails can make the difference between first and fifth place. Even if your sails are fresh out of the bag, you should be aware of the clues that show deterioration.

When looking at the tack or clew of a headsail, notice the reinforcing patches. They were glued and stitched together when the sail was first made. If they show stretch lines from the corner to the center of the sail, check for delamination. If you find it, look for stitches that have broken. Any of these symptoms are a sign to consult your sailmaker. Next, lay the sail out carefully on a lawn or in a parking lot and look carefully at each seam. If you find broken stitches and areas patched with ripstop, the sail should go back for repair. Check the luff tape, too. Quite often this will show a rip starting at the ends where the sail is fed into the luff groove. If the tape has been patched or there are any signs of tearing or broken stitching, the sail should be repaired.

When you get the sail back from the sailmaker, ask the sailmaker to sail with you to look at your inventory. Hoist each sail in turn, and take a careful look at its shape. Start with the leach: does it have a hook to it? Sails that have stretched usually stretch more in the middle. The leech and luff are comprised of more layers of sailcloth and stretch much less. This results in a hooked leech.

If the leech is open and flaps when the sail is used, you can remove a lot of the openness by tensioning the leech line. Drawing the leech line tight, however, often makes the leech cupped. If this is the case, the sail should be recut. To recut a sail, the sailmaker will usually remove stitches partway along the seams, adjust the panels, and resew the seams. He will then adjust the leech and luff curves and resew the leech. With these changes, your sail should last another season. The sailmaker will also give you an opinion on the content and quality of your entire inventory, telling you where there are gaps and what type of sail will fill them.

The next sail to look over is the mainsail. First check the batten pockets for wear and broken stitching; then look at the luff slugs, or carriages, and foot tape. Signs of corrosion or wear should be repaired as soon as possible. Check the leech tapes and leech line, and make sure that all the telltales are in place. Check each corner for signs of stress and delamination.

Hoist the sail and see if the sail shape has deepened. Usually a mainsail gets a fuller shape as it gets older, which means more heel and slower sailing. Older sails also show signs of stretching between the battens, where the leech starts to flap, and no amount of leech-line tension will remove the flapping. If this is happening to your sail, start looking for a new one.

When putting your sails away, make sure they are carefully rolled, folded, or flaked—don't just stuff them into a bag. Sails should be washed off with fresh water between races to remove salt water and make them less likely to absorb moisture. In a light-air race, lighter sails set better and make the boat faster. Only by keeping your sails in top shape will you have any hope of winning major races.

73: Rudders

What does the optimum rudder look like? That depends upon what you want to do. If you want high performance, you will want a rudder that has the least drag, highest lift, and minimum wetted surface. If you want to cruise, you will probably accept a sturdy rudder that can withstand lobster-pot buoy warps, and that will steer the boat well under all conditions.

The longer a rudder is, the less form resistance it has. Long, high-performance rudders are also narrow because a long, narrow rudder has less resistance than a short, wide one of similar area. Rudder thickness is a function of the blade width. A ratio of 8 to 10 percent of the rudder blade width is commonly used. If the thickness is smaller than 8 percent, the rudder usually will stall quickly, making turns difficult.

Some designers prefer the tip of the rudder to be gradually tapered, while others prefer a square tip. During my involvement with an America's Cup group, we noticed that tapered rudders seemed to generate smaller vortices that concentrated at the tip or where the rudder trailing edge swept forward. Keeping the trailing edge vortices small helps reduce the drag of the rudder. Some designers have recognized this and sweep the trailing edge of their rudders slightly aft to minimize vortex formation and subsequent drag.

All rudders should have a strong shaft or stock. After all, what use is a rudder if the stock snaps? Rudder stocks usually are made of aluminum or stainless steel alloys, with the blade formed around welded flanges. The space between the hull and the top of the rudder should leave just enough room for the rudder to clear the hull without touching it. Any more and you will lose efficiency as the water crosses over from one side of the blade to the other.

When you are buying a boat, try to find out how the rudder was built. If the flanges are welded on centerline to the stock, be aware that welding heats the metal, making this type of joint susceptible to breaking immediately behind the weldment. We once had exactly this type of failure on the way to Bermuda.

Fortunately, the rudder blade laminate held, which gave us a small amount of control. The laminate lasted long enough for us to get to the island.

The rudder blade must be as smooth as possible. A rough blade causes turbulence and reduces the rudder's efficiency. If you want the maximum performance from your rudder, try to get a template and make sure the rudder fits it precisely. It may require some work to get the rudder fair and smooth in both the horizontal and the vertical directions, but the results will be well worth it. Note that the leading edge of the rudder usually has a radius, or parabola, which will need to be preserved. Trailing edges are different: it is almost impossible to feather a trailing edge to a sharp point. You will find that you get as good a result if you terminate the trailing edge with a 1/8" or 3/16" (2 or 3mm) flat edge.

74: Understanding Lift and Drag

Sails generate lift. Keels and rudders generate lift. Even the hull of a boat generates some lift. Similarly, sails, keels, rudders, and hulls all experience drag.

Lift

Lift is generated by air or water passing over a suitably shaped surface. Airplane wings are highly efficient lifting surfaces, supporting the plane in the air by generating enough lift to overcome the weight of the plane. For example, Figure 74-1 shows the wing of a plane (A) set at an angle of incidence to the direction of the wind flow. (On a plane, this angle may be as low as 1 degree, but on a boat, the angle of incidence, or leeway, is usually between 4 and 7 degrees.) As the air passes over the wing, lift is generated by the difference in air pressure on both sides of the wing. Figure 74-1 also shows how the wing of the plane bears a strong resemblance to the keel of a modern sailboat (B). A keel and rudder of a boat move through the water at an angle of leeway. The leeway angle enables the keel to generate lift. Note that the hull also produces a small amount of lift. In a 12-meter, where the hull and keel are almost indistinguishable, hull-generated lift is over 60 percent of the total lift, but on a modern cruising boat, hull lift is less than 20 percent of the total lift.

The amount of lift an object generates is controlled by the shape of its surface and the angle at which it approaches the wind. Figure 74-2 shows how a

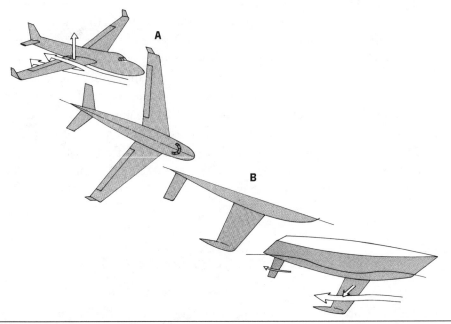

Figure 74-1: The keel of a boat performs a similar function to the wing of an airplane. The wings of an airplane generate lift and, in this sequence, the plane morphs into a boat. While the medium in which they operate changes, the characteristics of lift and drag stay the same.

Figure 74-2: As the angle of incidence increases along a keel or rudder, the waterflow breaks down, giving rise to a turbulent condition known as *stall*. When this happens, the keel or rudder is no longer generating lift.

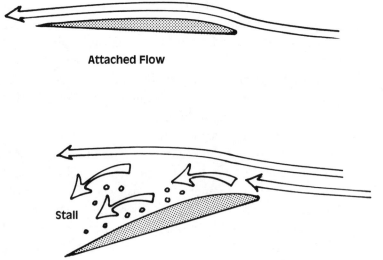

Attached Flow

Stall

wing's lift increases as the angle of attack increases, until the angle of attack is too high. At this point, the wing can no longer generate lift and is said to *stall*. Sails generate lift by their motion through the air. Sheeting a sail in too far has the same effect as increasing the angle of incidence of an airplane wing; the sail stalls.

On a keel, stall often occurs when the boat is spun through a tack too fast. Sailors can often feel the keel stall during a tack, as the boat slides sideways. The quickest way of getting out of a stalled keel situation is to ease the sheets and get the boat moving before heading up into the wind again. A rudder can also stall during a tack if it is put over too hard. In this case, stall can be felt as slowness through the tack. The best way of avoiding keel and rudder stall during a tack is to put the rudder over gently and steer the boat through the tack.

Drag

Drag, or resistance, can take many forms. The most well known is frictional drag, followed by wave-making drag and form drag. Frictional drag is the surface of the object coming in contact with the medium through which it is moving. For instance, every part of a boat in contact with the water experiences frictional drag, sometimes known as wetted-surface drag.

Frictional drag. The frictional drag defined above can develop in either laminar or turbulent flow. Laminar flow presents the least resistance and is achieved by obtaining the smoothest possible hull surfaces. If the surfaces are not smooth, or if there are abrupt variations in them, the waterflow becomes turbulent and drag increases.

Wave-making drag. When sailing in light winds, frictional drag comprises the largest part of overall drag. As the wind and boat speed increase, pressure waves rise around the hull, developing a form of resistance known as wave-making drag. As the distance between the wave crests increases, the drag increases until the boat can go no faster because it becomes locked in its own wave system, with one wave at the bow of the boat and another at the stern.

Form drag. Form drag is determined by the shape of an object. For instance, a round object, such as a ball, has much more drag than a streamlined object, such as a wing. Designers keep the appendages of a boat as thin as possible to reduce form drag. They can't make them too thin, however, because a thin keel or rudder stalls very easily and is difficult to mechanically fasten onto the hull.

On the Race Course

For many sailors, racing is the sole reason for going out on a boat: their relaxation, their catharsis, their entire recreation. Racing takes a tremendous amount of time and effort. I once calculated that I had raced about 60,000 miles over the last twenty years, most of it at speeds under seven and a half knots. At an average of six knots, that is 10,000 hours, or nearly 60 weeks of racing.

But for a racing sailor, time spent racing is nothing compared with the time that goes into preparing for the race, planning the race, studying tactics, post-mortems (usually in a comfortable bar or restaurant!), and sailing to and from the race. Each race is different, even if you have sailed the same course a hundred times. The wind strength is different, the tides are different, the crew is different, you might have a new boat. Good sailors learn something every time they go out on the race course; they also learn from reading books and watching racing videos.

75: Planning a Race: The Navigator's Job

You're ready to go racing. The keel, rudder, and hull have been sanded with 400 grit wet and dry emery paper, the sails have just come back from the sailmaker, the crew is hot to race, sandwiches are made—but from your electronic plot you suddenly find that the main compass is reading about ten degrees off. Swinging the compass is a minor job—it takes about an hour—but it is of major importance and is often forgotten in the rush to get everything else ready.

The navigator's first task in planning a race, without exception, is to read the race instructions. At this point you may also want to dig out the charts and mark every turning point. Also indicate if any buoys must be observed. Quite often, the race instructions will tell you that certain buoys—for example a wreck buoy—must be passed on the correct hand even though it is not part of the course. If the race is long, or part of it will be held overnight, the range of arcs of any lights should be drawn in with a compass.

The next step is to get the latest weather forecast. If your course takes you across a major tidal stream, such as the Gulf Stream, you will need a forecast for it. I prefer to get Gulf Stream forecasts several months in advance so that I can follow trends. (In one instance, I had four months' worth of stream plots on board and was convinced by observing the trends that an eddy had *not* moved the 40 miles that the forecasters were predicting. We aimed for the position indicated on my plots, while others went to the forecasted position and entered the eddy on the wrong side.) Check the tides for your area as well, and make a note of them. Remember to add in an additional hour for daylight saving time if necessary. For an afternoon race, get the weather forecast and mark the direction of the tidal stream.

For an afternoon race you probably won't bother working out estimated speeds and courses, but for an overnight race, laying out the course and estimating where the boat is likely to be for certain boat speeds can help you catch errors when you are tired and being bounced around at 4 a.m. For example, let's assume the wind is estimated at ten knots. For this wind speed, the boat speed will be six knots. Plot the entire course assuming the boat sails at that speed, then plot it for a boat speed of four knots, and make another plot for a boat speed of eight knots. In each case, mark when you will arrive at each turning mark. Let's assume your six-knot speed puts you at buoy number 2 at 1:06 a.m., and at buoy number 3 at 4:55 a.m. You arrive at buoy number 2 on time, and turn in for an hour of sleep. Suddenly at 4:10, the crew wakens you to say that buoy number 3 is on the horizon. Your first job is to check the log. If the wind and boat speed haven't changed, you know instantly that something is wrong. A quick check of the chart will show that another buoy has been mistaken for buoy number 3. Without having done your homework, you would have had to sit at the chart table and figure out where the boat was relative to buoy 3.

When you are laying out a course, show all tidal streams and indicate when they are likely to change. Also mark where the best water is likely to be. For instance, a rhumb-line course may take the boat under high bluffs which, given the weather forecast, provide a lee where the wind is likely to disappear.

On a long race, you will need to monitor weather reports constantly, so note weather radio station frequencies and their ranges in advance. You should also note harbors into which you can duck in the event of bad weather. A prudent navigator will carry charts for these harbors, in case you enter them under storm conditions and in darkness. Now that you have thoroughly prepared yourself for the race, you can go racing, knowing that your solid homework has given you every chance at winning.

76: At the Ten-Minute Gun

The class in front of you has started. You have watched their starts and have an idea where you want to start. You run the line from the committee boat to the other end and record the time taken. If you cannot run down the line because another class is starting, run it some distance behind the line, as shown in Figure 76-1. Take a bearing on the committee boat and sail until you get the same bearing on the buoy. Next, check the angle of the line to the course. It should be 90 degrees, but often one end or the other is favored. While you are performing these jobs, keep checking the wind speed and wind angle. Sometimes the wind angle will change just before a start, which will change all your calculations. If possible, check the tidal set and angle of the tidal stream.

By now you have checked and plotted any fluctuations in the wind speed and direction, run the line, and checked the course angle. With any luck you will have made a tentative guess at where you want to be when the gun goes off. To help you see if your position is good on the first leg, pick a boat that started in

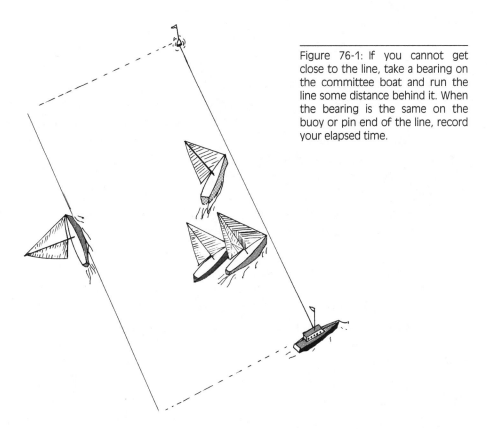

Figure 76-1: If you cannot get close to the line, take a bearing on the committee boat and run the line some distance behind it. When the bearing is the same on the buoy or pin end of the line, record your elapsed time.

the same place in the class ahead of you and see how it fares on the first leg. If that boat is doing well, you may have picked a solid starting position.

As you make your way upwind, after every tack, check the wind angle and write it down. This will accomplish three purposes. First, it will show you if the wind is fluctuating or varying in velocity. Second, it will show you if you are sailing on the same heading as an earlier tack in the same direction; quite often you will find that the wind will veer or back as you proceed down the course. Third, it will confirm your true wind angle calculation from the electronic instruments.

Before the ten-minute gun goes, record the time taken to perform a tack, from lee-ho to steady. Do the same thing for a gybe. These records will give you an idea of how long it will take to turn and head for the line. Pick a clear spot to make these maneuvers. If you try to perform them in heavy traffic you may get fouled out, or get your boat dinged up if an unexpected vessel appears under your headsail.

One thing that makes championship chess players better than average chess players is that they think eight or ten moves ahead; moderate players think only two or three moves ahead. If you want to sail a good race, you should figure out tactics for the entire first leg before you even start the race. The best start is the one in which you hit the starting line at full speed and know where you expect to be halfway up the first leg.

To make a good start, review all the factors you checked at the ten-minute gun and make sure you will be starting at the best position on the line. Typically, sailors start on starboard tack, but occasionally a port-tack start can pay off with big dividends.

The actual approach to the line can also be critical. Ideally, you should arrive at the line at full speed just when the gun goes. Arriving too early may force you to sail down the line or slow the boat to stay behind the line. Arriving too late may keep you in dirty air for the entire windward leg.

The Timed Start

In a timed start, the approach to the line is made by starting a certain distance behind the line at a predetermined time. Go to the starting line, note the time, and then sail away from it on a definite course for one to three minutes. If you sail for less than a minute you will not have time to make the turn, come back, and get up to speed on the approach to the line. If you sail for longer than three minutes and the wind dies, you could be stuck some distance from the starting line. Ideally, the course away from the line should be the reciprocal of the close-hauled course back to the line, but you may need to sail up or down a little, depending on wind fluctuation. Figure 77-1 shows the technique.

When you gybe or tack the boat, note the time taken to make the turn. Take your time on the first attempt to the starting line. Note the wind strength, the course, and the wind angle. When you hit the line, make a note of your time. If you start your approach sequence to the starting line at the ten-minute gun, you will have enough time to make two practice approaches.

At every turn, check the wind speed and angle to make sure there are no late fluctuations. When making your final approach, make sure you are not too high at the end of your run. It is better to sail a little low early in the run than be forced to turn away at the committee boat because you are high and trying

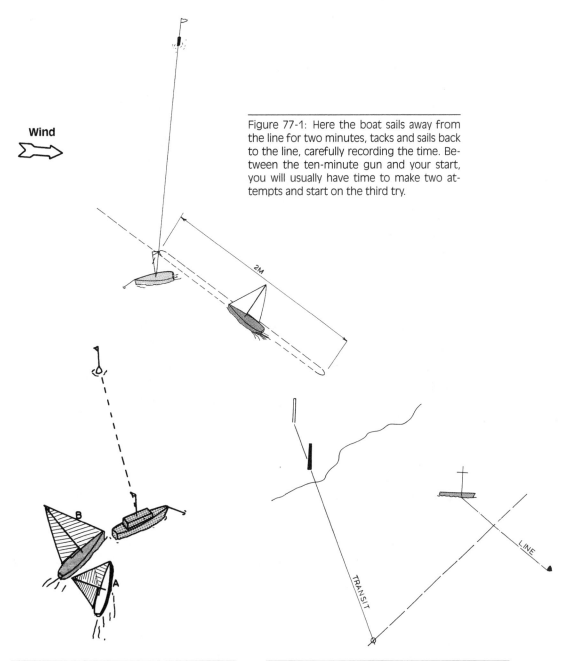

Wind

Figure 77-1: Here the boat sails away from the line for two minutes, tacks and sails back to the line, carefully recording the time. Between the ten-minute gun and your start, you will usually have time to make two attempts and start on the third try.

2M

Figure 77-2: Don't sail high of the line and hope you can barge your way in. Chances are there will be a boat in the way that will shut the door on you, as boat B is doing to boat A.

TRANSIT

LINE

Figure 77-3: Here tall chimneys on shore are being used as a transit point. By sailing from the line to the transit, the navigator has established that it will take, say, two minutes to reach the line. The boat should be at the transit point at precisely two minutes before the start.

to dive low (or barge) to cross the starting line, as boat A is doing in Figure 77-2. However, if you are laying the committee boat and a boat above you is trying to barge its way in, you are perfectly within your rights to luff them to windward of the committee boat, as long as they are not mast abeam of you.

Starting Close to Shore

Currents and tides make starting lines close to shore trickier, but they can also be easier because the marks are fixed on shore, allowing you to select a landmark and time your run for the line perfectly. When starting a race close to shore, first check the tidal stream. If it is against you, make sure to approach with enough speed to overcome it. An alternative is to approach the line from above and allow the tide to push you below it at the outer end, then harden up and sail across the line. If the tide is going in the same direction as the course, you will have to make a longer approach so that you are not carried across early.

Having sailed along the line and recorded how much time it takes, select where you are going to start, then find a landmark on shore from which you can time your start. Make your practice approach and note the time from the landmark to the starting line, as shown in Figure 77-3. Repeat the procedure to make sure your timing is accurate. Check to see if the tide is getting stronger or weaker: You could throw off your timing if you forget changes in tidal strength.

78: Getting the Favored Position at the Line

The optimum starting position is not always at the windward end of the starting line, at the committee boat, with the rest of the fleet under you. If the line is biased, or if port tack is favored, you may find that a port-tack starting boat can cross the entire fleet and get ahead of you.

The favored position at the start line is the one that puts you in front halfway up the first leg of the course. From the front, you should then be able to fend off the rest of the fleet. In Figure 78-1 the boat at the windward end of the line (F) has the best start, as it arrives at the line just as the gun goes. It has mast abeam on the boats to leeward so they cannot luff. In Figure 78-2 the leeward-most boat (A) has luffing rights over the boat above it, which means

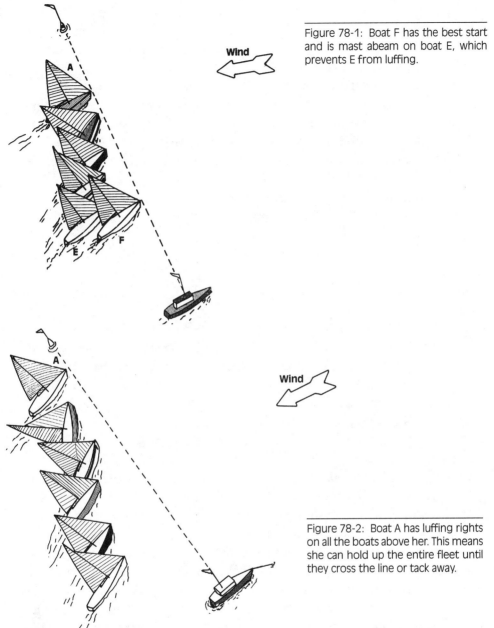

Figure 78-1: Boat F has the best start and is mast abeam on boat E, which prevents E from luffing.

Wind

Figure 78-2: Boat A has luffing rights on all the boats above her. This means she can hold up the entire fleet until they cross the line or tack away.

that A controls the line. If boats above it try to bear off, then A can hold them all up and force them to go over early or tack if they have room.

Check other classes that started in front of you. Check potential wind shifts.

You might want to get on the course early and sail the first part of the weather leg. The race committee for the Royal Yacht Squadron in Cowes, for example, would always send the fleet in the direction of the tidal stream to clear the starting line for the next class to start.

In races around Narragansett Bay in Rhode Island, on the other hand, the race committee almost always starts the fleet to windward. As the prevailing wind is southerly, most of the time the course will be to the south.

Both of these starting points have areas where the wind swirls and eddies around land masses, which can give the smart sailor an advantage. Thus, the ideal position on the starting line is often the one that gets you to the lift or header first. If you know where the header is, you can sail fast, with sheets just cracked, and tack over into the lead, instead of holding high and taking longer to get to the header.

79: Windward Leg Tactics

Prior to the start of the race, decide where you want to be halfway up the first leg. This will influence your starting position. Having started, there are three major requirements for sailing the windward leg: clear air, clear air, and clear air. You cannot go fast if you are sailing in another boat's backwind. If you can get the other boats to sail in your backwind, they'll be sailing slower.

This means that you should watch the class ahead, or watch the smoke and flags onshore, to see if there are wind shifts down the course. Constantly check the bearings of the other boats in your class to see if they are moving faster or picking up a wind shift. Also note your boat's heading on each tack. This will tell you whether the wind is veering or backing over a longer period than a single tack, and will add more strategic information to your stockpile.

If you spot a shift, stand on into a header, then tack. This will give you a lift on the other tack. If you are lifted, stay on the same tack until the lift becomes a header and then tack. If the lift keeps lifting (known to racing sailors as "sailing a great circle course") and you have to tack for the mark, you will have picked the wrong side of the course. Ideally, you should have spotted this lift before you sailed into it, and tacked early to make it a header on the other tack.

Before tacking, check other boats around you to make sure you are not about to tack into a wind shadow. Constantly monitor your instruments to check the wind angle and the favored tack angle. The entire object of the windward leg to is to maximize VMG (speed made good to windward). Nothing else matters except getting to the windward mark first. Here are some rules of thumb that help in most situations.

1. Duck starboard-tack boats, which have the right of way, if they are one-half to two-thirds of a boat length ahead of you. If they are slightly closer, or one-third to one-half of a boat length ahead of you, tack under them and work your way clear, unless the other side of the course is favored.
2. Never sail to the port layline unless there is a major wind shift that favors that side of the course.
3. Sail to the starboard layline as late as possible in terms of the tactical situation. Ideally, you should arrive at the starboard layline about 10 to 20 boat-lengths from the mark. If you leave it too late and approach the buoy on port, you will probably have to duck several boats. If you get there too early—20 boat-lengths away from the mark, for example—you may get a wind-shift and fall below the mark, or have to stand on further to avoid getting dirty air from a boat ahead.
4. Always try to give boats behind you dirty wind. The bad air effect from your sails lasts for about 12 to 20 boat-lengths, depending on the wind strength. At a turning mark, dirty wind can cause the boat behind you to pinch for the mark and sail slowly, giving you more of a lead.
5. If you are behind, try to figure a course that keeps you out of dirty air without taking a flyer. Usually, the boats at the front are sailing the best course and the best way to the mark is to follow them. Unfortunately, that puts you in their wind shadow. Often, the only way to get back in contention is to take a flyer and hope you can catch up. Most of the time, flyers will hurt.

80: Checklist for Best Speed to Windward

Keel and Rudder
- Smooth and faired; the smoother the keel and rudder, the higher the lift and the lower the frictional drag.
- Optimum shape. The keel and rudder shapes should be the optimum for the style of boat or class.

- Rudder close to hull with minimal gap. If weed or a line gets trapped between the rudder and the hull, it will slow the boat.

Hull

- Faired properly; like the keel and rudder, the hull should be smooth and faired for lowest frictional drag.
- Clean; a dirty hull is slow, even if it has only a thin layer of slime on it.
- No abrupt changes in shape; a sharp joint or lump, such as a depth transducer protruding out of the bottom of the hull, can stimulate turbulence and slow the boat.

Headsail

- Check wind strength and correct sail for wind speed. Many sailors try to carry a light headsail into a stronger wind. Not only does this slow the boat, it also can ruin the light headsail. Make sure the sail is changed at the right time.
- Make sure the luff tension on the sail is correct for the wind strength. Set the sails up with no wrinkles, then adjust the headstay and halyard tension to suit the wind and wave conditions.
- A hooked leech is slow, so make sure that there is correct tension on the halyard and the leech of the sail. Adjust the genoa sheet lead if the leech tension is too tight, or ease the leech line. If neither works, get a qualified sailmaker to look at the sail and recut it if necessary.
- Make sure the sheet lead is in the optimum position. Check all sets of telltales and any leech telltales. Also check that the slot between the mainsail and genoa is sufficiently open. In light winds you may have to use an outboard lead, which will need to be brought inboard or barber-hauled as the wind increases slightly. As the wind gets even stronger, you will have to move the lead outboard again before changing to a smaller sail.
- Constantly check the telltales to make sure they are flying properly.

Mainsail

- Just like the genoa, the mainsail luff tension should be set up properly. Tighten the halyard until there are no wrinkles in the sail. You will have to adjust the halyard if wind strength changes.
- Adjust the leech tension on the mainsail with the leech line. If the line is too tight it will cause the leech to hook. If it's too loose, the leech will flap.

- Check the position of the outhaul. This control flattens the lower third of the sail. Keep it tensioned so that the bottom part of the sail is full, without wrinkles. If the outhaul is too tight, a horizontal crease will usually appear just above the boom.
- Adjust the sheet and vang tension so that the mainsail telltales are flying straight out. You may find that the top telltale is hard to keep flying straight. The problem is that the mast causes turbulent flow across the sail, which keeps the telltale in disturbed air flow.
- When the telltales are flying properly, the battens should be in the ideal position. Check from under the boom to make sure they are just right. When they are optimum, the top and bottom battens point about 10 degrees above the centerline of the boom and the middle battens are either just below or parallel to the centerline of the boom.
- Check the position of the steering wheel quite often. If the helmsman has more than a quarter-turn of wheel on, you may need to ease the traveler down the track slightly.

Crew

All too often on racing sailboats, the members of the crew are sitting on the rail and facing outboard watching other boats, or focusing their attention on something outside their own boat. The primary job of the crew is to make sure their boat is sailing fast: their weight should be on the rail and they should be watching their boat's sail trim and offering suggestions to the afterguard. They should also be watching for puffs and eddies in the wind, and looking at boats in other classes for changes in wind direction. In Long Island Sound or Narragansett Bay, for instance, the early morning wind is often from the north, but during the course of the day it usually shifts to the south. By anticipating the wind-shift long before it happens, you can prepare another sail, or tack to get into the new wind quickly and steal a few boat-lengths on the opposition.

When the crewmen are on the rail, they should move as little as possible in light winds. This will enable the sails and hull to settle down and the boat to sail faster. In *very* light winds, the crew weight should also be farther forward and to leeward to get the wetted surface of the stern up out of the water slightly and make the boat sail faster.

When you are on a final beat and it looks as if the wind is slightly stronger to the right-hand side of the course, do you head toward the wind and leave the boat following you with a straight shot at the finish line, or do you stay between the second boat and the finish line? If you want to win the race, stay between any boats behind you and the finish line. That is the primary rule for finishing a race. If you can slow the boats astern of you, so much the better.

How do you slow another boat? The most common method is to stay upwind of a following boat, as shown in Figure 81-1. Tacking on top of another boat is a good way to make sure the boat behind you is receiving dirty air off your sails. If the wind is reasonably strong and you are in a match race with another boat, you can sometimes allow your mainsail to flap: This disturbs the air behind you and is effective in slowing a following boat, but it will also slow your boat. If there are other boats on the course, sail as fast as you possibly can and keep the other boats in your wind shadow.

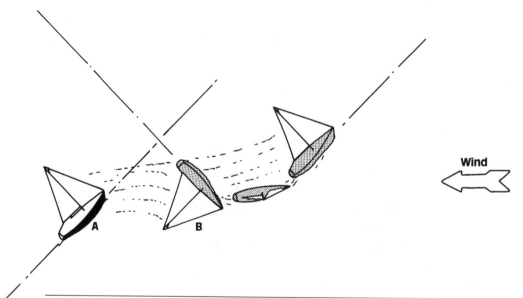

Figure 81-1: Boat B crosses in front of boat A and tacks on top of it. This puts boat A in B's wind shadow. Boat A must either drive off to get to leeward of B's wind shadow or tack away. This is a typical sequence of events in a match race. By tacking on top of another boat, you can drive it to one side of the course or the other.

By knowing the racing rules you also can use aggressive tactics to win a regatta. Suppose you have raced a week-long series and on the day of the final race, the second boat needs to get a second or third place to beat you. You might decide to sail alongside the second boat and keep that boat from getting a good fleet position. One famous helmsman was well known for sailing aggressively against other boats that challenged his dominance. In one race, he sailed his opponent right off to the side of the course, giving the opponent a last place.

Another way to win a race is to control where your opponents can sail. To do this, make sure you get a good start and then cover your opponents during every leg of the course. Sailing to windward, you might try to keep your opponents on one side of the course by tacking on top of their boats every time they try to get to the other side.

82: Windward Mark Rounding

If you race in a closely matched fleet, such as the J24, then you will have experienced the frustration of approaching the mark on port and finding no gap between the next ten starboard-tack boats, forcing you to tack behind them. Unless there is a major advantage to approaching from port, you should always try to approach the windward mark on starboard tack. Figure 82-1 shows what can happen if you come in from the port side. Boat A will just be able to tack and get ahead of boats D and E, but boats B and C will have to duck D and E. After the mark, the order will be A, D, E, C, and B.

Stay wide on the approach and then turn so that the boat

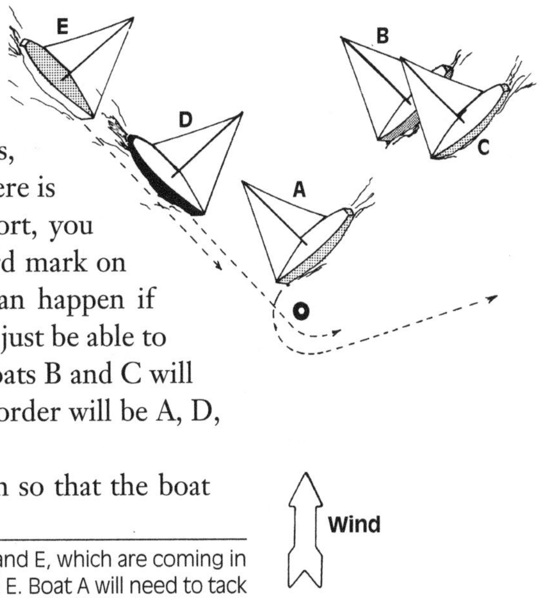

Wind

Figure 82-1: Boat A will tack and get ahead of boats D and E, which are coming in on starboard, but boats B and C will have to duck D and E. Boat A will need to tack and come onto a reach after turning the mark; this could slow boat A considerably and allow boat D to climb into an advantageous position. After the mark, the order will be A followed closely by D and E, then by C and B.

will be very close to the mark as you leave it. If you approach it close and swing wide as you leave it, you leave a space for a following boat to get between you and the mark as you pass it. This following boat could get an overlap and prevent you from tacking or gybing on the next leg.

If you do not have an experienced crew, take the time to go through each job with each crewman. Make sure that all the people on board know their job when they have to execute it, and approximately how much line or sail they have to pull in. Make sure they also know when to *stop* doing their job. In other words, make sure they know when to stop hauling on a sheet or sail.

Note that the racing rules change when boats come within two boat-lengths of the mark. A boat behind you with an inside overlap can call for room, and you must give it at the turn. If there is no overlap, you are free to sail your own course. If there is likely to be any discussion of the point, somebody on the leading boat should check the overlap as the boats near the mark and call to the other boat that no overlap exists. Should the following boat attempt to get inside you and you go into the protest room, the fact that you called "no overlap" should win the protest.

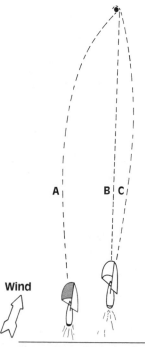

Figure 83-1: If B is the rhumb-line course, the boat sailing course C will come into the mark at reaching speed, while A will sail the last third of the leg dead downwind. Sailing dead downwind is very slow.

83: Downwind Leg Tactics

You have rounded the windward mark and are now sailing downwind. If you are not in the lead, what is the next best position? First, never sail dead downwind in light winds. In the polar diagrams in Figures 91-1 and 91-2, you will see that at no time do the apparent wind polars show the boat sailing faster dead downwind. The fastest point of sail is always on a broad reach. If you are not sure where the boat's best VMG (Velocity Made Good—a combination of boat speed and wind angle when sailing downwind) is, keep the wind arrow between the four- and five-o'-clock position. Sail higher in lighter winds (in very light winds you might need to keep the wind on the beam), and further aft in heavier winds. If you record the wind speed, wind angle, and boat speed data for these positions, you will eventually be able to develop your own VMG polar charts.

Of course, sailing on a broad reach means that you will have to gybe. When setting up the best position in which to gybe, keep the following points in mind:

1. Try not to sail to the layline early in the leg. If you get out on a layline and the wind shifts, you may have to run dead downwind to the turning mark.
2. Gybe only as often as needed, no more.
3. Try to set up your course to approach the leeward mark on starboard gybe, unless the wind angle indicates otherwise.
4. Watch boats ahead for wind shifts and the favored side of course.
5. Try not to let an opponent climb onto your wind. Remember, however, that a larger boat will pass you, so there is little point in trying to luff a larger boat. If a larger boat is going to pass you, simply drive off a little and get further away from it.
6. If a smaller boat is about to pass you, you are either sailing badly or should consider luffing the smaller boat. Remember that when you luff another boat, both boats lose distance. If you are fleet racing and the passing boat doesn't affect your standings, sail lower and away from it and let it go. If the other boat will beat you on points if it passes you, and your other opponents are a long way behind, you should luff.
7. Try not to sail high of the mark early in the leg. If you go high you will have to sail downwind during the latter part of the course, and dead downwind is slow. In Figure 83-1, the boat that is sailing course A will have to sail slowly dead downwind in the last third of the leg. The boat that is sailing course C will come into the turning mark at reaching speed.

84: Slowing Your Opponent Downwind

You have been racing for three hours and your opponent clearly is faster upwind. Both boats have rounded the weather mark and are heading downwind. You need to catch your opponent and put some distance between the two of you before you head upwind again. How can you do this? You know your op-

Figure 84-1: Boat B is
blocking the wind from
reaching boat A. This has
the effect of slowing
boat A.

Wind

ponent will be watching, so your first job is to take stock of the positions of other boats around your opponent's boat. If there are boats to weather of it, you might want to set a course so that it will come up to cover you and get sucked into the bad air of a third boat, as shown in Figure 84-1. You might also try to get an opponent's boat to stand out into a less advantageous tidal stream. When sailing in the Solent, for example, it pays to have a knowledgeable sailor on board who can set a course that keeps your boat just inside an adverse current, but forces your opponents to stand into the current to cover you.

If you are only a short distance behind your opponent's boat, you could try to attack its airstream—that is, position your sails directly upwind from him. Depending upon the wind speed, your wind shadow can carry for up to 20 boat-lengths downwind from your boat.

85: Checklist for Best Offwind Speed

First make sure that the keel or centerboard and rudder have been raised. This reduces wetted surface and makes the boat faster off the wind. The only time you might want to leave them down when sailing downwind is in heavy air. Also check over the side to make sure no lines or sails are trailing in the water.

The sails are critical for offwind speed. Make sure the spinnaker is of the right weight to suit the conditions, that it has no holes, and that the leeches are not curled. (If a spinnaker has been overused, quite often the cloth stretches and causes the leech tapes to curl.)

When using the sail, square the spinnaker pole to the wind. Make sure that the pole is even with or slightly lower than the other spinnaker clew. (If you cannot see the other clew, look at the centerline seam; it should be vertical.)

The spinnaker leads should be as far outboard as possible to project the maximum sail area. Easing the sheet as far as possible will also help project sail area.

Consider if a staysail tacked to the windward rail and set under the spinnaker can help clear the stagnant air out from behind the mainsail and increase boat speed. Under certain conditions, I've found that a well-set staysail can increase speed by an additional quarter of a knot.

When sailing downwind, the mainsail becomes a wind-blocking device instead of a lifting surface. Shape is not so critical but projected area is. Make sure that the projected sail area is maximized by easing the mainsheet, traveler, and vang, and by putting the boom at right angles to the apparent wind.

The crew weight should be aft in most conditions. The only time crew weight forward will help is in very light, ghosting conditions. As the wind speed increases, the crew weight should be moved farther aft to keep the rudder immersed and the stern in the water.

86: Rounding the Leeward Mark

The best time to decide where you want to be on the next leg is while you are still making the approach to the leeward mark. For instance, if the mark is to be left to port, and the favored side of the course is off to starboard after you have rounded, you will not need to tack after rounding. Thus, making tactical moves to shake off an overlapping boat and stop it from rounding inside you is not as critical as it would be if you had to tack immediately after rounding. This leaves you plenty of time to figure out where you want to be on the next leg. Having decided that, the decisions on the best approach to the mark, how to round, when to take down the spinnaker, and so forth should all fall into place. Figure 86-1 shows a typical situation at the leeward mark. Boat A is on the outside and slightly behind boat B. Boat B rounds the mark wide, leaving plenty of room for boat A to slip astern and come out of the tack in a controlling position.

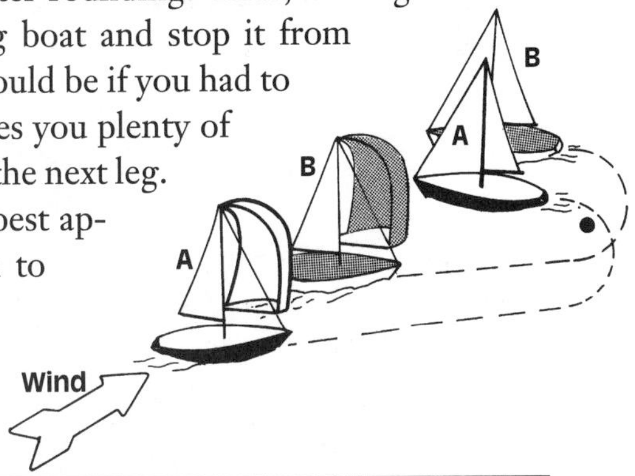

Figure 86-1: Boat A is on the outside and slightly astern of boat B. As they round the mark, boat B goes wide and lets A slip in. Boat A emerges from the tack in a controlling position. Boat B cannot tack until A tacks away.

As an example, let's say that the leeward mark is followed by a windward beat, and the wind is likely to shift to the right, or starboard, side as you make your way up the weather leg. You decide that you need to put in a short hitch to the left after rounding and then tack back to get to the probable wind shift. As you approach the mark, tell your crew that you are going to tack immediately after rounding the mark. The foredeck crew must get everything clear quickly.

Discuss the takedown with the crew and make sure everybody clearly understands his job. The crewmen who are to drop the pole and get the topping lift off are particularly important. You should also make sure that the foredeck crew checks that the genoa sheets are over the top of the spinnaker pole and ready to run freely during the tack. If you miss this important step, the sheets can snarl, delaying the tack or stopping the boat.

As you near the mark, check for nearby boats that could cause problems and, if necessary, assign a person to determine if there is an overlap. Get the spinnaker down quickly, and stay clear of the mark on the approach. Round the mark so that you are close to it as you come out of the turn. That way, you will gain a yard or two to windward after rounding. As soon as the spinnaker is unclipped from the pole, drop the outboard end of the pole on deck and unhook the topping lift. When the topping lift is clear, the boat can be tacked. It doesn't matter if the spinnaker is not all the way down; it can be gathered later. Tack over and clean up. As soon as the boat has settled on the next course, the foredeck crew can go back to cleaning up the deck and repacking the spinnaker.

87: Reaching Leg Tactics

When sailing on a reach, the shortest distance along the leg is a straight line between the two turning marks, but tactical considerations may cause you to sail above or below the rhumb line. For instance, a wind-shift ahead that turns the reach into more of a run may make you decide to sail low in the early part of the leg, and reach up later to keep up your boat speed. When reaching, you should try not to climb high early in the leg. While going high may seem fast early on, it can turn deadly slow when you have to run down to the mark, and the boats below you continue to reach up close to maximum speed.

Because all sailboats with similar waterline lengths sailing on a reach tend to move at close to the same speed, passing on a reaching leg is difficult. Larger boats, with their tendency to go faster, usually sail right past smaller boats. If you are about to be passed by a larger boat, the best protection is to climb high before the larger yacht gets near you, and let it pass downwind of you.

If you are sailing the two reaching legs of an Olympic triangle, your reaching tactics toward the wing mark should be aimed at making sure you have an inside overlap at the mark. This will help you pass the boat on which you have an overlap and improve your position in the fleet. Also make sure you have an inside overlap at the leeward mark, so that you can prevent any boat outside you from tacking after the leeward mark has been passed.

88: Approaching the Finish Line

All too often the crew starts to lose its racing edge as the boat approaches the finish line. Having won several races by a few seconds (in one recent race, the first 11 boats finished within 13 seconds of one another), I have learned that it is crucial to sail as fast as possible right past the finish line. When nearing the finish, approach the line sailing fast and keep sailing fast until the entire boat has crossed the finish line. You'll hear the gun if you are first across.

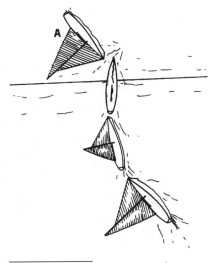

Try to approach the finish line on starboard tack so that you have right of way over any port-tack boats. As you get near, take bearings or estimates to figure out if the line is skewed and which end is favored. If you have been recording the boat's headings on each tack, you will quickly be able to determine when you have neared the layline for the pin or committee boat. This will let you know when you can tack and lay the finish line.

Figure 88-1: Here the boat has "shot" the line to save a few seconds as it crosses. Boat A shows an optional position if you do not want to tack.

A boat typically sails at a true wind angle of 35 to 45 degrees to the wind, and the race committee tries to put the line at 90 degrees to the wind. You'll get across the line faster if you can hit it at 90 degrees, so you should "shoot" the line as soon as your boat's bow hits it. Figure 88-1 shows how to bring the bow up and shoot the line. The boat should have plenty of speed to carry it across.

Once you are over the finish line, get clear of it to allow other boats to cross, then clean up your boat. I always like to get the boat cleaned and gear stowed before breaking out drinks or sandwiches.

89: Using Tidal Set to Your Advantage

If you have ever sailed off Egypt Point, in the Solent, or through the Race at the end of Long Island Sound, you'll have experienced firsthand how fast the tide can run. Using the tide direction to your advantage can improve your performance on the race course. Here are a few pointers.

First, make sure you have checked the tide tables and added an hour for daylight saving time where necessary. Then check to see where the strongest tide is running. If the tide is going with you, position your boat in the strongest tide. If the tide is against you, try to find shelter on top of shallow spots or behind headlands, and if possible locate favorable eddies. In one coastal race off Portland Bill, we went inshore; other boats stayed out in the channel in the belief that the tide would be weaker in the middle of the English Channel. We stayed just close enough inshore to pick up a back eddy, stayed in the eddy until the last minute, and ducked into Lyme Bay. By the time we had crossed the bay to the next headland, the tide had changed. I learned subsequently that the eddy we had sailed in was only there at a certain state of tide. Had we been there an hour later, we would also have had to go offshore.

Most sailors' biggest fear is having to cross a strong tidal current in light winds, but this need not be a disadvantage. The strength of a two-knot tide pushing the boat into the wind increases the true wind strength by two knots. With the right combination of sails and a little luck, you may be able to turn that into a gain in apparent wind that gets you across the tidal stream fairly quickly.

90: Understanding the Wind Triangle

True wind, apparent wind, heading, and *leeway;* these are the terms used by experienced sailors to get around the race course. What do they all mean?

True wind is the wind you feel when you are standing still. For instance, if you were to go outside right now and stand still, you would be able to easily determine the direction of the wind, and, with a relatively simple instrument, its speed.

If you got into your car and drove against the direction of the true wind with your hand out of the window, you would feel an apparent wind on your hand blowing stronger than the true wind, and the direction of your car would be called its heading. The apparent wind strength would be the true wind strength plus the speed of your car. For instance, if the true wind was blowing out of the south at 10 miles an hour, and you drove your car south at 25 miles an hour, your car's heading would be south, and you would feel an apparent wind speed of 35 miles an hour from the south.

If you drove north at 25 miles an hour, you would feel an apparent wind speed of 15 miles an hour from the north, even though the true wind would still blow from the south. Apparent wind, then, is a combination of the direction and speed of the true wind and the direction and speed of the object from which the wind is being measured. These measurements are easy to make when the boat or car is heading in the same direction as, or in the opposite direction from the true wind; they are more complicated in other circumstances. The problem is illustrated in Figure 90-1.

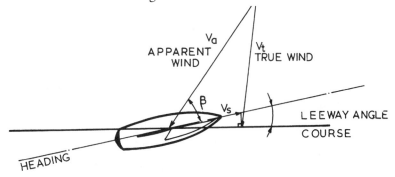

Figure 90-1: The wind triangle. The boat is sailing along a heading and making leeway. True wind is the wind the boat will experience when the vessel is standing still, but the boat's forward motion tends to make the apparent wind appear farther forward.

When you are racing you do not want to stop time after time to measure the true wind. The vessel's on-board instruments, which measure the apparent wind speed and direction and the boat's speed and direction can all be used to mathematically determine the true wind. But there is an added complication: unlike cars, boats make leeway, which is the difference between a boat's course and its heading. Using the car example again, suppose you were heading south and hit a patch of ice, the hood of the car points southeast, but the car is still going south, so it could be said the car is making a temporary leeway angle. Leeway can vary from 3 or 4 degrees for a 12-meter to 7 to 9 degrees for a cruising boat. The leeway angle is very difficult to measure accurately. Instrument manufacturers usually assume a number given the type of boat.

91: Sail-Potential and Polar Plots

Is there a polar plot in your future? Polar plots, or polar charts as they are often called, can take several forms. The first and most basic is a chart of the type of sails that are on board and the wind angles and strengths in which they are used. Figure 91-1 is a typical plot showing types of sails and their effective ranges. This chart is a good indicator of what may be missing from your sail inventory. It can also indicate the optimum conditions under which to change a sail or when reef it. To make a chart like this, you need to keep careful notes. Every time you change a sail, note the wind angle, wind speed, and reasons for the sail change. After a few cruises or races, you should have enough information to fill out the chart.

Figure 91-2 is a sail-potential polar chart developed by using the on-board instruments and some form of data recorder, such as a portable computer. When this chart is used in conjunction with the sail inventory chart in Figure 91-1, you should have a good sense of the potential performance of your sail wardrobe, where the gaps are, and when to use each sail. As sails get older, you will also be able to check their performance deterioration.

To make a polar chart, make sure your instruments are accurate and then sail through a number of different wind angles with each type of sail. Plot the boat speed, wind speed, and wind angle for each sail at 5- or 10-degree intervals. For sails with a very narrow range, record the information at 5-degree intervals; you can record spinnaker information at 10- or even 15-degree intervals. To obtain data, sail a steady course for 5 or 10 minutes, then start to take read-

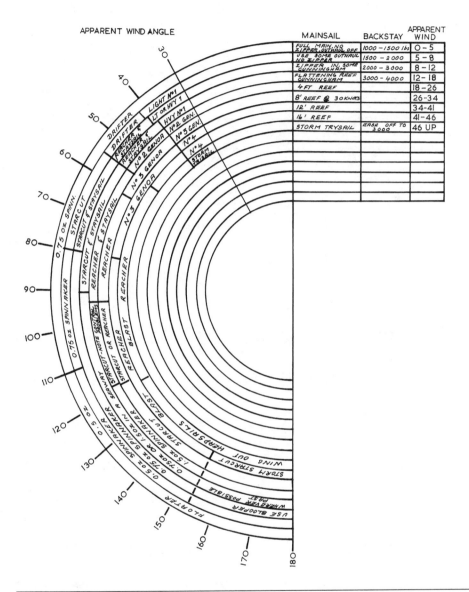

MAINSAIL	BACKSTAY	APPARENT WIND
FULL MAIN, NO ZIPPER, OUTHAUL OFF	1000 - 1500 lbs	0 - 5
USE SOME OUTHAUL, NO ZIPPER	1500 - 2000	5 - 8
ZIPPER IN, SOME CUNNINGHAM	2000 - 3000	8 - 12
FLATTENING REEF, CUNNINGHAM	3000 - 4000	12 - 18
4 FT REEF		18 - 26
8' REEF @ 30 KNOTS		26 - 34
12' REEF		34 - 41
16' REEF		41 - 46
STORM TRYSAIL	EASE OFF TO 3000	46 UP

Figure 91-1: A sail-potential plot. This plot lists every type of sail carried on board, and the wind speed and angle over which it can be carried. Note that this plot lists many more sails than most boats carry.

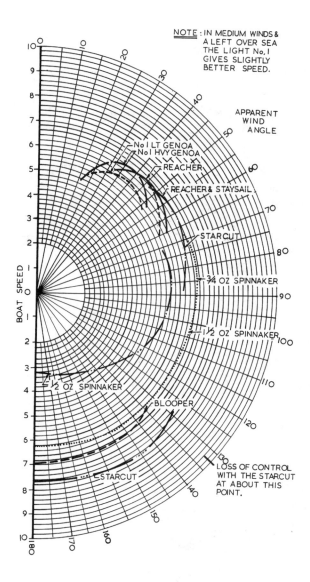

Figure 91-2: A sail-potential polar plot. This plot shows the potential speed of each sail in your inventory and the range over which it can be carried as actually recorded by on-board instruments. In a way, this plot is more accurate than the one in Figure 91-1, in that it tells you what the sails are capable of on your particular boat. It also shows you gaps in your inventory.

ings. Continue to take readings for 10 to 20 minutes. Sail down 10 degrees and repeat the performance. Come down another 10 degrees and do it again. While this sounds tedious, it is the most accurate method of obtaining information about each type of sail.

92: Developing Polar Plots

True wind polar charts and apparent wind polar charts show the potential of the hull in certain wind speeds for every point of sail. Either chart can be developed from the other, but for most sailing needs the true wind polars are the most useful. Figure 92-1 shows typical true and apparent wind polar charts.

If you want the best true wind polar plots for your boat, you will have to develop them from actual sailing conditions on the boat. That is, you will have to put a full crew on board, go out sailing and record the wind speed and direction and boat speed and direction for every point of sail and wind strength. Fortunately, many computer programs can use the data generated from several sailing trips and interpolate information to fill in the blank spots. Still, these types of charts cost time and money to make, and because the crew is not sailing during an actual race, the charts may show slower speeds than they would if they were taken under racing conditions.

To cut down the time and cost of making polar plots, you may be able to obtain a plot developed for the International Measurement System (IMS). The IMS uses boat speed information to determine the handicap of specific boats. This information can also be used to develop a full set of polar diagrams. There are certain limitations, however: your boat must either be measured for or be in one of the classes for which the IMS has developed records. There is a fee for this service. Contact your local rating authority for more information. The local rating authorities may be the local yacht club; an organization recognized by the American Sailing Association, formerly USYRU; a PHRF committee; a MHS committee; and many more.

The IMS plots are a place to start, but you should also keep meticulous records while you are on the racecourse. The best way to do this is to use a computer to record information. This information can then be used to upgrade the IMS data, and to make sure that any new sails you acquire operate as efficiently as possible.

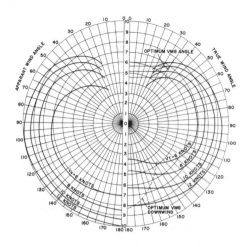

Figure 92-1: True and apparent wind polar plots.

93: Using Polar Plots

Using a polar plot is quite simple. You simply select a suitable wind strength and determine on the chart the boat speed for a given wind angle. For instance, in Figure 93-1 a polar chart section shows the performance of a boat sailing to windward. For the best speed to windward, project a horizontal line across from the boat speed figure (along the center of the chart). The point at which this line touches the boat speed curve is known as the optimum VMG (Velocity Made Good), the optimum speed and wind angle on the windward leg.

You can also draw a similar horizontal line for downwind sailing and determine the optimum VMG points for downwind sailing. When selecting the best wind angle for sailing downwind, you should sail at the best VMG angle and gybe as often as needed. This will get you downwind faster than sailing dead downwind. Notice how, in the true wind polar chart, the boat is sailing much slower when it is heading directly downwind than when it is sailing at the optimum VMG. The extra speed more than compensates for the extra distance sailed, provided your gybes are executed properly.

An example of this is a race I sailed in the Championship of the Mediterranean. As darkness fell, the wind died to one or two knots. We moved the

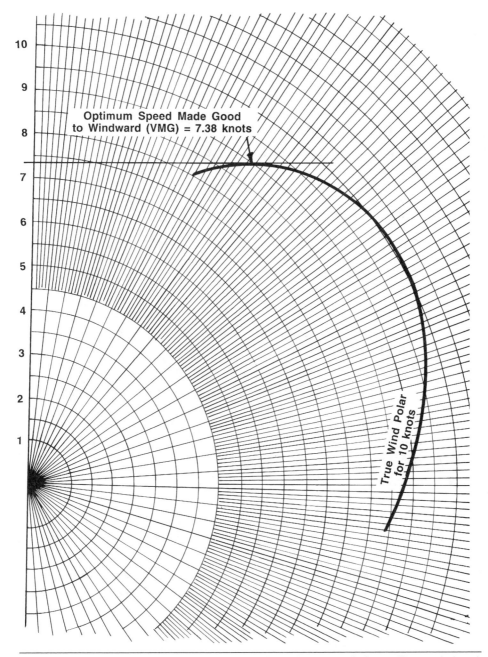

Figure 93-1: The section of a polar plot that shows the performance of a boat sailing to windward. By using this area of the chart you can determine the boat's best velocity made good to windward (VMG).

spinnaker pole forward and reached off at a 60-degree angle to the other boats in our class. We sailed fast for about two hours, gybed, and came back to the fleet. On the first pass we had gained about 600 yards on the class, and by morning the rest of our class was hull down behind us. As the wind filled in later in the day, we were able to sail to the finish line well ahead of our class.

When you are racing, a polar chart is also useful for projecting your course on subsequent legs of the race. For instance, if you are sailing on one leg and need to know what sail to set on the next leg, you can determine the true wind speed and direction from the velocity triangle, and extract the required sail information from the polar chart.

94: Using Your Wind and Boat Speed Instruments to Best Advantage

The sailor who watches the wind instruments and compass constantly is following the performance of the boat. But instruments record what has happened, not what is about to happen. When you are sailing, you should be able to sense what is about to happen and make appropriate corrections beforehand. If the bow swings off to port slightly, for example, you should be able to feel that turn and correct it before the problem becomes acute. If you are watching the compass, there is a time lag between the bow swinging to port and the compass recording it. By the time you see the swing on the compass, you have to make a much larger correction to get the boat back on course.

Used properly, however, instruments can be very helpful. The most frequently used instrument is the boat-speed indicator. When sailing to windward, combining boat speed with apparent wind angle and wind speed can immediately tell you whether the boat is going faster because the wind has increased or lifted, or because the helmsman has sailed off onto a reach. The best method of checking the cause of boat-speed change is to watch the true wind angle and speed. This separates boat speed from the apparent wind triangle and makes the changes easier to detect. You should also make a note of the compass course to detect lifts and headers early.

When sailing downwind, the wind angle indicator tells you if the boat is sailing at the best wind angle to maximize speed. For instance, in Figure 92-1, the best downwind VMG is obtained at about 160 degrees in 10 knots of true wind. If the boat is held at 160 degrees, the speed indicator should show a speed of about 6.7 knots. If the speed drops, check the wind angle and wind speed, and then the sails.

The wind instruments can also indicate sail changes. If the sailmaker says a certain sail should be changed at 15 knots, use your own judgement about whether or not to make the change then. First, determine whether the sailmaker means true or apparent wind. Fifteen knots of true wind can be a lot more or less than apparent wind, depending upon the wind angle. Then check out the sea state. In general, you should change sails earlier in a lumpy seaway than in flat water. Tactical considerations may keep you from making the change. For instance, if you are tied in a race with another boat and both yachts are heading for the finish line, you probably won't want to make a sail change if the wind increases a few knots.

Using wind instruments properly is just one part of the overall instrument picture. You might also use Loran or GPS for positioning and navigation, a depth sounder, and even a portable computer to evaluate your sailing performance. Whatever instruments you use, be sure to read the instructions and understand how that instrument can help you sail better and faster.

PART THREE

EMERGENCY!

Basic Emergency Techniques

W hat do you do in an emergency? In America, most people yell for the Coast Guard. In Britain, the coast guard and the world renowned Royal National Lifeboat Institution (RNLI) come to your aid. Other countries have their own rescue services. On the high seas, the nearest country will usually coordinate rescue attempts, and any ship in the area will aid a mariner in distress.

At one time, high-seas rescues were difficult. Your chances of rescue depended on whether another ship was in the area to receive your radio-transmitted SOS. Today, satellite systems tremendously enhance your chances of survival. In the BOC single-handed around-the-world races, for instance, contestants carry Emergency Position Indicating Radio Beacons (EPIRBs), known as Argos for constant monitoring. (Argos can send and receive up to 16 messages via satellite. EPIRBs can only be used in an emergency.) Inmarsat (International Marine Satellite, a satellite radio-telephone link) is the latest innovation. Should any contestant now get into trouble, the Inmarsat or the onboard EPIRB system can provide the authorities with the boat's position immediately.

Systems such as these have made offshore sailing safer, but sailors who clutter up emergency channels with chit-chat and use emergency systems for minor assistance put other sailors at risk. Remember that emergency channels are for emergencies only. Cluttering the airwaves with discussions of places to moor or wind strengths in your area may be blocking out a genuine emergency call.

95: Calling for Help

The most common way to call for assistance is by radio. Few sailors fly flags upside down or carry emergency flags. If they do, they are more likely to be called fools by passing boats for flying their flag upside down than to attract help.

The most common radio used in coastal waters is the VHF (Very High Frequency) radio. This radio is said to have "line-of-sight capabilities," which means that if you can see the person or boat to whom you are transmitting, your message will get through. To maximize the range, the antenna should be at the masthead rather than on deck. Over longer distances, a VHF radio may not have the capability to deliver clear communications. For longer distances, use a single-sideband radio (SSB) that operates in the medium frequency (MF) range. Single-sideband radios have ranges up to 600 miles, and your message should get through, barring exceptional atmospheric conditions.

EPIRBs are not used as ordinary radios. They are activated only in an emergency. To activate an EPIRB, the ground plate must be in the water and the battery turned on. The EPIRB emits a signal that can be picked up by satellite or airplane and enables rescuers to locate the beacon. A marooned sailor should never turn off the EPIRB to conserve battery power; rescuers need to home in on the beacon's signal.

VHF

In an emergency, first make sure the radio is tuned to channel 16 (156.8 MHz), the international emergency channel monitored by the U.S. Coast Guard and the U.K. coast guard. In the U.S., almost anyone at sea can and does use the VHF radio. All that is required is a station license from the Federal Communications Commission (FCC) and an annual fee. The FCC license is good for five years. In the UK, the VHF may be used only by a person who is qualified by the Maritime Radio Service to use the set.

A typical VHF set operates on 12 volts and has three or four dial controls for squelch, channel select, and volume. To use the set, the operator holds the microphone close to his or her mouth, presses the microphone button, and speaks. Because VHF sets are usually "simplex" sets, the operator cannot hear other people when transmitting and must say "over" at the end of each transmission.

Unless other arrangements are made, all calls should be initiated on channel 16 and promptly switched to another channel as soon as contact is established. In the U.S., channels 9, 68, 70, and 72 are recreational intership and ship-to-ship channels, and channels 69, 71, and 78 are ship-to-shore channels. Many marinas and boatyards monitor channel 69 for incoming visitors. In the U.K., ship-to-ship channels are 6 and 8, and port operations are on channels 12 and 14.

When initiating a call, the procedure is quite straightforward. Let's say your boat is called *Tiger Too* and you are calling another boat called *Zephyr* to set up a rendezvous. Switch to channel 16 and wait for a break in the conversation. Then say clearly:

"Hello, *Zephyr*. This is *Tiger Too*. This is *Tiger Too*. Over." You can repeat your boat's name up to three times.

Zephyr replies, "Hello *Tiger Too*. This is *Zephyr*. Over."

Your reply should be: "Hello *Zephyr*. Go to channel 72. Over."

Both operators switch to channel 72.

You transmit. "Hello *Zephyr*. This is *Tiger Too*. Over."

Zephyr replies: "Hello *Tiger Too*. This is *Zephyr*. Over."

From here you can continue with a normal conversation, but remember that other people may be waiting to use the airwaves, so keep your conversations short.

In a dire emergency, your transmission will be different. Preface every call with MAYDAY. Then give the yacht's position and the type of emergency.

For instance, for an emergency call to the Coast Guard, pick up the microphone and say clearly, "MAYDAY MAYDAY MAYDAY. This is the yacht *Tiger Too*. We are seven miles due east of Point Judith. We are sinking fast. Over."

The Coast Guard will reply: "Yacht *Tiger Too*. This is the Coast Guard." Upon hearing the words MAYDAY MAYDAY MAYDAY, the Coast Guard will clear the channel if other transmissions can be heard. The Coast Guard will then ask for an accurate position, the type of emergency, how many people are on board and a description of the boat. You may be told to set off flares or distinguish the vessel in some way. You may also be asked to shift to another channel to keep the emergency channel clear. The Coast Guard may ask for other vessels in the area to identify themselves and come to your aid. Once the vessels have identified themselves, the Coast Guard will coordinate rescue efforts and may dispatch its own boats or helicopters to the scene.

At sea there is no stronger signal than MAYDAY MAYDAY MAYDAY. If you broadcast those words, a large organization swings into action. If you send a frivolous or bogus mayday message, you can be fined, sentenced to jail, or ordered to pay the costs of the rescue forces that responded.

If your message is urgent but not an emergency, you can broadcast a "pan" call. For instance, if your boat is dismasted but not in danger of sinking, you may want to send an urgent message to the Coast Guard. In this instance, transmit "PAN-PAN PAN-PAN. This is *Tiger Too.* We have been dismasted seven miles due east of Point Judith. Nobody is hurt. We will head for Newport."

At that point, the Coast Guard will request your position and vessel identification. If you cannot get underway, they may dispatch a towing service operator such as SeaTow.

Note that some of the newest radios have what is called a "voice-synthesized mayday capability." You simply press a button (which can be located anywhere on the vessel) and the mayday radio unit transmits an emergency message automatically. When the mayday unit is linked to a Loran or GPS unit, it also transmits the vessel's identification and its exact position. The message continues at regular intervals until either the microphone's talk button is depressed or it is shut off.

Single Sideband or Medium Frequency (SSB or MF)

The emergency channel on Single Sideband or Medium Frequency (SSB or MF) is 2182 kHz. This channel should be used in a manner similar to that described for VHF. Always try the frequency first and resort to SSB for emergency calls only if necessary.

Argos is the name of a satellite-based system that has been in operation since 1978. The on-board Argos unit can transmit up to 16 messages—including the user's latitude and longitude position, the date and time the message was sent to and received by the satellite, and the ambient temperature around the user's unit, as well as the state of the user unit's battery—to one of two orbiting satellites monitored by the National Oceanographic and Atmospheric Administration (NOAA). Although the NOAA provide world-wide coverage, two satellites messages can take up to one hour to be received, depending upon the position of the user on the earth's surface.

96: Harnesses, Life Jackets, and Life Rafts

Wearing a life jacket can save your life, especially if you are a nonswimmer who loves to sail. When buying a life jacket, make sure it is Coast Guard approved and meets their standards (see Appendix A for the properties required by the U.S. Coast Guard).

When you don your life jacket, make sure that all the straps are done up, including the strap under the crotch. Read the instructions and wear the jacket properly. If you don't, the life jacket could simply slip over your head, or worse still, jerk upward and break your neck when you jump off the boat. Make sure the whistle and strobe light work.

When not in use, your life jacket should be stored flat in a dry place. Too often, life jackets are simply crammed into a locker and forgotten. When they are needed they are often torn, or mildewed, or smell stale, and in some cases they are rotten with age. If you invest in a good life jacket, it should be stored where you can reach it easily in an emergency and where it can lie flat without heavy objects on top of it. Occasionally, you should pull out your life jackets and inflate them hard. Any that do not remain inflated should be returned to the manufacturer for repair or discarded. At the end of every season or two, return your jackets to the manufacturer for checking and repair.

Wear your life jacket if you are a nonswimmer, if you are an inexperienced sailor, if you are performing a risky job on the boat, or if you feel the jacket will give you confidence to move around. A life jacket is not a sign of weakness, and you should feel at ease wearing one. In an emergency, don your life jacket first, then attend to the emergency.

97: What to Do if You Fall Overboard

When I fell over the side, we were gybing a racing boat and were about 15 miles from the nearest land. As I clipped the lazy guy onto the spinnaker, the sail filled and I was lifted off the deck into the ocean. I realized that it was up to me to swim. But which way? Fortunately, the crew had tossed a life ring over the side with its pole and drogue, so I swam toward that. It took the boat 24 minutes to return. (The crew said they had to vote whether to come back!) They couldn't see me in the water (it was late afternoon), but did see the man-overboard pole and aimed for it. As they neared the pole, they spotted me and maneuvered to pick me up. For the first time, floating alongside, I realized how big and heavy the hull of a boat is.

My experience was fortunate. We had a good crew who knew what to do. If you happen to fall over the side, here are a few pointers:

1. Remove heavy clothes, but do not remove all your clothes. A layer of clothing next to your body will help you keep warm.
2. Try to float or swim slowly without expending much energy. The longer you can float, the better your chances of rescue.
3. If you are wearing a life jacket, keep it on and float with it. Don't fight it trying to swim and don't remove it, *especially* if the water is cold; just curl into a ball and float. Life expectancy in 40-degree water is very short—less than an hour for most people. By curling up, you keep most of your body warmer. More people die because of hypothermia than from any other water-related cause. (Other than drunk driving on the water.)
4. When the rescue vessel approaches, make sure you get the crew's attention. Wave, blow your whistle, shout, or do whatever it takes to get noticed. People in the water are very hard to spot.

98: Getting a Person Out of the Water

Rescuing someone from the water is a hard job. Usually, the person has little strength left to climb onto the boat and the people on board will have to haul him or her out. Here are some common methods:

1. Lower the steps and help the person to climb up. Sometimes the person in the water can climb the steps alone.
2. Make a rope sling or use a life ring to lift the person out. I saw one crew undo the shackle pin on the mainsheet, put the person into a sling hooked to the lower tackle on the mainsheet, and haul away. If you decide to use this method, you may have to reeve a line to hold the boom out over the side of the boat.

3. Use the main halyard hooked to a sling to get the person out of the water. As the halyard is pulling from the centerline of the yacht, the person in the water will be pulled against the side of the hull. You will need to fend the person off from the side of the boat while he or she is being hauled on board. Also, never wrap a halyard or sheet around the person in the water and haul away. The tension of the halyard or sheet around the heavy, water-laden person could injure ribs or lungs.
4. If the person cannot get into a sling, you will have to resort to more drastic measures, one of which is to leave the mainsail on the boom, but lower the top portion of the sail into the water. The person in the water then swims into the bight of the sail and is hauled up using the main halyard. The problem with this method is that the person in the sail can slide back out into the water.

    You can also use the genoa to get a person out of the water in a similar manner, but you should tension the foot of the genoa by sheeting it in before lowering the sail over the side.
5. Yet another method is for a person on board the boat to get into the dinghy and pull the swimmer into it. In the dinghy, the swimmer could recover for a few minutes before climbing on board. You will, however, have to be careful not to capsize the dinghy during the operation.
6. The last method is to use a halyard run through the end of a spinnaker pole. This keeps the person in the water away from the hull and lets the person on board maneuver the pole to lower the person onto the foredeck.

99: Making Up a Grab Bag

Sailors going on the BOC single-handed around-the-world race must by rule have a grab bag on board in case their boat sinks and they have to be rescued. Sailors going on a long cruise may want to invest in a similar bag for emergencies. A life raft is equipped with a certain number of items for survival, but a grab bag can hold many more items and could make the difference between survival and death.

For the BOC racers, the grab bag must contain the following, over and above what is stored on the life raft:

1. Clothing for warmth and protection

2. A waterproof flashlight
3. Two white flares, two red flares, and two orange smoke signals
4. Two dye markers
5. Spare containers of water or solar stills for making fresh water
6. Emergency food rations and vitamin tablets
7. Sunscreen and sunburn lotion
8. Fishing tackle
9. A sharp knife

In addition to these items, you might want to add extra gear from the following list:

1. A lightweight "space blanket." This thin blanket with foil on one side directs lost heat back toward your body. It was developed by NASA, hence the name
2. A box with a couple of chemical light sticks, spare batteries, fishing jigs and hooks of various sizes, and fishing line of about 20- or 25-pound test
3. A mirror
4. Spare plastic bags for storing dry clothing
5. Chocolate bars or dried rations
6. A small strobe light with spare batteries
7. A baler and a sponge
8. A spare chart of your cruising area, a pencil, eraser, dividers and, if you can find room, two small triangles
9. A can/bottle opener
10. A spare watch or radio

The grab bag itself should be of a waterproof material and have many pockets. Don't load up the grab bag with a huge number of items, but try to supplement the gear in the life raft. It may seem as though you'll never need it, but if you are going to embark on a long cruise, a grab bag should be part of your planning.

100: Man-Overboard Drills

Quite often when we were returning from a race, somebody would suggest a man-overboard drill to the helmsman, yell "Man overboard!" and toss a cushion over the side. We would then go into a man-overboard drill to pick up the cushion. Man-overboard drills are useful only when they are a surprise and are constantly practiced.

The object of the man-overboard drill is to get the boat back to the object in the water as quickly as possible. This means the sail may have to be dropped, the engine turned on, and lines pulled in before the boat can make its turn.

A well-organized man-overboard procedure has several components. The first is for one person to step up to the side of the boat and spot the man in the water. It is very easy to lose sight of a person's head in the ocean, so spotting should be that person's only job.

The remainder of the crew should drop the life ring and pole, and get the boat turned around. If sails are set, the headsails will probably need to be dropped. Dropping them on deck is fine, as long as all sheets and lines are inboard and not trailing. A trailing line can easily get hooked around the prop.

If you do not motor back, you will need to gybe or tack the boat to get to the person in the water as fast as possible along a reciprocal course. While gybing is faster, the situation may call for you to tack fast instead. Most methods for getting the boat turned around quickly require good coordination between crew and helmsman.

Approach the person in the water from downwind and aim to position the boat slightly upwind of him or her. The boat will drift faster than the man in the water, making the approach fairly easy. If you are motoring, remember to take the prop out of gear, but leave the engine running. Once the boat is near the person in the water, a line or several lines can be thrown and the person pulled alongside if he or she is conscious. If the person is unconscious, a crew member onboard may have to go into the water to get a line around the person overboard. The second person going overboard should wear a line to avoid being swept away from the boat and the person in need of rescue.

101: First Aid Checklist

First aid kits can be purchased as a complete package or can be made up from the following list of components. If you want to buy a full kit, consider the kits developed by Medical Seapak Company (see Appendix B). These kits have almost everything you are likely to need for seaborne first aid.

Close to Shore Kit

Adhesive strips (Band-Aids)
Sterile cotton wadding
Gauze bandages
Elastic bandages
Eye pads
Adhesive tape
Zinc oxide ointment
Motion sickness tablets or motion bands
Sterile wound wipes
Aspirin or nonaspirin pain reliever
Tweezers
Scissors
Sunscreen (SPF 15)
Sunburn cream
Fish hook remover kit

Offshore Kit

All of the items at left, plus:
Forceps
2" and 4" gauze bandages
2" and 4" elastic bandages
Abdominal pads
Gauze pads
Iodine wipes
Cold pack
Triangular bandages
Butterfly closures
Eye irrigation kit
Ammonia inhalants
Extra rolls of adhesive tape
First aid booklet
Rescue blanket
Rubber gloves
Inflatable splint
Scalpel or very sharp knife
Burn and scald relief kit
Antibiotic ointment
Dental kit

Check with your family doctor before going to sea on a long cruise. If necessary, you might need to add prescription medications and other items suggested by your doctor.

Sailors planning a long offshore cruise should take a CPR course and a basic first aid course before going to sea.

Appendix A

U.S. Coast Guard Life Jacket Standards

Type I PFD
- must support 22 pounds positive buoyancy.
- must turn an unconscious person face up from a face-down position
- is acceptable for all boats
- is recommended for offshore cruising

Type II PFD
- must turn an unconscious person face up
- must support 15.5 pounds of buoyancy
- is recommended for coastal cruising
- is acceptable for all boats

Type III PFD
- must support a conscious person in an upright position.
- must have at least 15.5 pounds of buoyancy.
- is recommended for in-the-water sports, on lakes, or close to shorelines
- is acceptable for boats of all sizes

Type IV PFD
- is a throwable, not worn, device.
- must have 16.5 pounds of positive buoyancy
- is acceptable for boats less than 16 feet, such as canoes and dinghies
- is acceptable as a throwable device for boats over 16 feet

Boats 16 feet or over must have one Type I, II, or III device for each person on board, and one Type IV device in the boat.

Boats smaller than 16 feet must have one Type I, II, III or IV device for each person on board.

Appendix B

Addresses of Manufacturers of Safety Equipment

Heatpak Industries, Inc.
409 Harding Industrial Dr.
Nashville, TN 37211
Tel: (615) 831-0234
Fax: (615) 831-0218

Liferaft & Survival Equipment, Inc.
One Maritime Dr.
Portsmouth, RI 02871
Tel: (800) 451-2127 or (401) 683-0307
Fax: (401) 683-2875

Medical Seapak Company
1945 Ridge Rd. E.
Suite 105
Rochester, NY 14622
Tel: (800) 832-6054
Fax: (716) 266-3222

Offshore Survival Products
Box 190
Hawthorne, FL 32640
Tel: (800) 707-8823

Port Supply/Lifesling
Port Supply
500 Westridge Dr.
Watsonville, CA 95076
Tel: (408) 761-4270
Fax: (408) 728-3014

**PUR, Division of
Recovery Engineering, Inc.**
2229 Edgewood Ave. S.
Minneapolis, MN 55426
Tel: (800) 548-0406
Fax: (612) 541-1313

Quality Marine Products, Inc.
4880 Church Ln.
Galesville, MD 20765
Tel: (301) 867-1462
Fax: (301) 867-7139

School of Survival Specialities, Inc.
N. 3808 Sullivan Bldg.
Spokane, WA 99216

Sporting Lives, Inc.
P.O. Box 518
Meridian, ID 83642
Tel: (208) 888-4184

Survival Technologies Group
6418 U.S. Highway 41 N.
Suite 266
Apollo Beach, FL 33572
Tel: (800) 525-2747
Fax: (813) 641-1110

Survival Products, Inc.
5614 S.W. 25 St.
Hollywood, Fl 33023
Tel: (305) 966-7329
Fax: (305) 966-7329

Life Raft & Survival Equipment, Inc.
One Maritime Dr.
Portsmouth, RI 02871
Tel: (800) 451-2127 or (401) 683-0307
Fax: (401) 683-2875

Neptune Research
2611 Old Okeechobee Rd.
Suite 3
W. Palm Beach, FL 33409
Tel: (407) 683-6992
Fax: (407) 683-8366

Offshore Survival Products
P.O. Box 190
Hawthorne, FL 32640
Tel: (800) SOS-TUBE

Switlik Parachute
P.O. Box 1328
Trenton, NJ 08607
Tel: (609) 587-3300
Fax: (609) 586-6647

Cal-June
5238 Vineland Ave.
N. Hollywood, CA 91601
Tel: (818) 761-3516

Cruising Gear
2751 S.W. 27th Ave.
Miami, FL 33133
Tel: (305) 854-7600
Fax: (305) 854-5984

Genco Sails
544 King St. W.
Toronto, Ontario M5V 1M3
CANADA
Tel: (416) 364-2891
Fax: (416) 364-6635

Helly Hansen (US), Inc.
17275 N.E. 67th Ct.
Redmond, WA 98078-9731
Tel: (800) 435-5901
Fax: (206) 885-3882

Holland Yacht Equipment
P.O. Box 452
San Carlos, CA 94070
Tel: (415) 595-2009
Fax: (415) 592-6627

Indiana Mills & Mfg.
18881 US 31 N.
Westfield, IN 46074
Tel: (317) 896-9531
Fax: (317) 896-2142

Lirakis Harness
18 Sheffield Ave.
Newport, RI 02840
Tel: (800) USA-SFTY
Fax: (401) 846-5359

MRC (Mariner Resource)
86 Orchard Beach Blvd.
Port Washington, NY 11050
Tel: (800) 645-6516
Fax: (516) 767-7835

Musto, Inc.
333 West 76th St.
New York, NY 10023
Tel: (212) 580-3653
Fax: (212) 799-3395

Nautical Technologies, Ltd.
217 Burliegh Rd.
Bangor, ME 04401
Tel: (207) 942-4751

Raudaschl Sails Canada
3140 Lakeshore Blvd. W.
Toronto, Ontario M8V 1L4
CANADA
Tel: (416) 255-3431
Fax: (416) 259-9136
Harnesses and bosun's chairs

Survival Technologies Group
6418 U.S. Highway 41 N.
Suite 266
Apollo Beach, FL 33572
Tel: (800) 525-2747
Fax: (813) 641-1110

Life Jackets

L. L. Bean
Casco St.
Freeport, Me 04033
Tel: (800) 221-4221

Douglas Gill USA
Div. Weathermark
6087 Holiday Rd.
Buford, GA 30518
Tel: (404) 945-0788

Eastern Aero Marine
3850 N.W. 25th St.
Miami, FL 33142
Tel: (305) 871-4050
Fax: (305) 871-7873

Extrasport
5305 N.W. 35th Ct.
Miami, FL 33142
Tel: (305) 633-2945
Fax: (305) 633-0837
Life vests

Harishok
R.R. 2, Box 922

Old Grafton Tpk.
Canaan, NH 03741
Tel/Fax: (603) 523-7363
Life jackets

Jim Buoy
A Division of Cal-June, Inc.
P.O. Box 9551
North Hollywood, CA 91609-1551
Tel: (213) 761-3516
Life rings, PFDs, horseshoes, floats, and buoys

Kent Sporting Goods
433 Park Ave.
New London, OH 44851
Tel: (800) 537-2970
Fax: (419) 929-1769
PFDs, life jackets, and cushions

Mustang META USA Corp.
3870 Mustang Way
Bellingham, WA 98226
Tel: (206) 676-1782
Fax: (206) 676-5014

Northwest River Supplies
2009 South Main St.
Moscow, ID 83843
Tel: (800) 635-5202 or (208) 882-2383
Fax: (208) 883-4787

O'Brien International
14615 N. E. 91st St.
Redmond, WA 98052
Tel: (206) 881-5900
Fax: (206) 883-7378
Waterski life jackets

Omega Marine Products
1638 Parker Ave.
Fort Lee, NJ 07024
Tel: (800) 966-6342
Fax: (201) 943-9053

Safegard
P.O. Box 2044
Covington, KY 41012

Tel: (606) 431-7650
Fax: (606) 431-1355

Sporting Lives
P.O. Box 518
Meridian, ID 83642
Tel: (208) 888-4184
Fax: (208) 888-4267
Suspenders, inflatable life preservers

Stearns Mfg. Co.
P.O. Box 1498
St. Cloud, MN 56302
Tel: (612) 252-1642
Fax: (612) 252-4425

Stormy Seas, Inc.
P.O. Box 1570
Poulsbo, WA 98370
Tel: (800) 323-7367 or (206) 779-4439
Fax: (206) 779-8171
Makers of jackets with inflatable cells built-in

Survival Technologies Group
6418 U.S. Highway 41 N.
Suite 266
Apollo Beach, FL 33572
Tel: (800) 525-2747
Fax: (813) 641-1110

Switlik Parachute
P.O. Box 1328
Trenton, NJ 08607
Tel: (609) 587-3300
Fax: (609) 586-6647

Viking Life-Saving Equipment (America)
1625 N. Miami Ave.
Miami, FL 33136
Tel: (305) 374-5115

Wellington Puritan Mills
Monticello Hwy.
Madison, GA 30650
Tel: (800) 221-5054

Fax: (706) 314-0407

West Marine Products
500 West Ridge Dr.
Watsonville, CA 95076-4100
Tel: (408) 728-2700

Liferafts

SMR Technologies, Inc.
P.O. Box 326
1420 Wolf Creek Trail
Sharon Center, OH 44274
Tel: (216) 239-1000
Fax: (216) 239-1352

Avon Inflatables/Liferafts
1851 McGaw Ave.
Irvine, CA 92714
Tel: (714) 250-0880
Fax: (714) 250-0740

Chase, Leavitt & Co., Inc.
10 Dana St.
Portland, ME 04112
Tel: (800) 638-8906
In ME (800) 244-0675

Datrex, Inc.
P.O. Box 1150
Kinder, LA 70648-1150
Tel: (318) 738-4511
Fax: (318) 738-5675

Dunlop-Beaufort Canada
12351 Bridgeport Rd.
Richmond, British Columbia V6V 1J4
CANADA
Tel: (604) 278-3221
Fax: (604) 278-7812

Eastern Aero Marine
3850 N.W. 25th St.
Miami, FL 33142
Tel: (305) 871-4050
Fax: (305) 871-7873

Givens Ocean Survival Systems Co., Inc.
1–8 Lagoon Rd.
Tiverton, RI 02871
Tel: (800) 328-8050 or (401) 683-7400

Imtra
30 Barnet Blvd.
New Bedford, MA 02745
Tel: (508) 990-2700
Fax: (508) 994-4919

Offshore Repack and Repair
10 Industrial Pk.
P.O. Box 155
Essex, CT 06426
Tel: (800) 243-1176 or (203) 767-8293

Outfitters USA Services, Inc.
1111 Ingleside Rd.
Norfolk, VA 23502
Tel: (800) 727-BOAT) or (804) 855-2233

Revere Survival Products
603–607 West 29th St.
New York, NY 10001
Tel: (212) 736-5400
Fax: (212) 629-8039

Seaco/Elliot
3874 Fiscal Ct.
Rivera Beach, FL 33404
Tel: (407) 842-8900
Fax: (407) 842-0987

SMR Technologies, Inc.
P.O. Box 326
1420 Wolf Creek Trail
Sharon Center, OH 44274-0326
Tel: (216) 239-1000
Fax: (216) 239-1352

Switlik Parachute Co., Inc.
P.O. Box 1328
1325 East State St.
Trenton, NJ 08607
Tel: (609) 587-3300
Fax: (609) 586-6647

USA Outfitters Services, Inc.
326 First St.
Annapolis, MD 21403
Tel: (410) 626-1122
Life raft repacking, sales and service

Viking Life-Saving Equipment (America)
16Z5 N. Miami Ave.
Miami, FL 33136
Tel: (305) 374-5115

Winslow Marine Products
928 S. Tamiani Trail
P.O. Box 888
Osprey, FL 34229
Tel: (813) 966-9791
Fax: (813) 966-6887

Yachting Services
P.O. Box 1045
Pointe Claire, Quebec H9S 4H9
CANADA
Tel: (514) 697-6952
Fax: (514) 695-5912

Zodiac of North America
P.O. Box 400
Thompson Creek Rd.
Stevensville, MD 21666
Tel: (301) 643-4141
Fax: (301) 643-4491

Manufacturers of Anchors and Anchor-handling Gear

Canor Plarex
P.O. Box 33765
Seattle, WA 98133
Tel: (206) 621-9209
Fax: (206) 340-8845

Creative Marine
P.O. Box 2120
Natchez, MS 39121
Tel: (800) 824-0355

Crosby Co.
183 Pratt St.
Buffalo, NY 14240-1083
Tel: (716) 852-3522
Fax: (716) 852-3526

Down Under Marine
P.O. Box 3216
Clearwater, FL 34630-8216
Tel: (813) 585-0023
Fax: (813) 584-3112

Hans C-Anchor, Inc.
P.O. Box 66756
St. Petersburg, FL 33736
Tel: (813) 867-4645
Fax: (813) 867-6797

Hathaway, Reiser & Raymond
184 Selleck St.
Stamford, CT 06902
Tel: (203) 324-9581
Fax: (203) 348-3057

Imtra
30 Barnet Blvd.
New Bedford, MA 02745
Tel: (508) 995-7000
Fax: (508) 998-5359

Paul E. Luke
Box 816

E. Boothbay, ME 04544
Tel: (207) 633-4971
Fax: (207) 633-3388

Mooring, Inc.
Box 60204
Houston, TX 77205
Tel: (713) 443-8229

Nav-X Corp.
1386 West McNab Rd.
Ft. Lauderdale, FL 33309
Tel: (800) 825-NAVX or (305) 978-9988
Fax: (305) 974-5378

Para-Tech Engineering Co.
10770 Rockville "B"
Santee, CA 92071
Tel: (619) 448-1189
Fax: (619) 448-3059

Rule Industries
70 Blanchard Rd.
Burlington, MA 01803
Tel: (617) 272-7400
Fax: (617) 272-0920

Shewmon, Inc.
1000 Harbor Lake Dr.
Safety Harbor, FL 34695
Tel: (813) 447-0091

Simpson-Lawrence USA, Inc.
3004 29th Ave, E.
Bradenton, FL 34208
Tel: (813) 746-7161
Fax: (813) 746-7166

SRS Anchor Co.
708 S. Euclid Ave.
Bay City, MI 48706
Tel: (517) 686-2540
Fax: (517) 667-0070

Index

cable-laid, 13
catenary of, 21
chafing of, 23
checking of, 23–25
frayed, 61
nylon, 18, 21, 35
shackles for, 24–25
size of, 18
water depth and, 21–22, 25–26
see also chain
Lirakis harness, 6–7
Lloyd's Register of Shipping, 18
lockers, 13, 114
locks, 60
LOFT program, 126
logs:
  maintenance, 119–20
  navigational, 144
  performance, 124
Long Island Sound, 60, 153, 162
Loran, 109, 171, 177
luffing, 148–49, 157
lunch hook, 35

"made," 94
mainmast, 56, 132, 133
mainsail:
  in docking and mooring, 78, 81
  flattened, 133, 134
  gybing with, 89–90
  mainmast and, 132–33
  reefing of, 95–96
  in rescue operations, 179–80
  setting and trimming of, 42–43, 49, 52, 53, 57, 58, 71–75, 87, 89–90, 94, 116, 135, 152, 154
maintenance log, 119–20
"Man overboard!," 181–82
marinas, 30, 31, 60, 65–66, 79–83
Maritime Radio System, 176
marlin spike, 23
masthead, 118, 131
masts:
  aluminum, 117
  bending of, 132–33
  controls of, 134–35
  hauling of, 110
  longitudinal tuning of, 132–33
  raking of, 133
  removal of, 115
  transverse tuning of, 130–32

tuning of, 124
mast step, 133
mast wedges, 130, 131
matches, 4
MAYDAY, 176–77
meat, 61
Medical Seapack Company, 182
MF (Medium Frequency) radio, 177
mid-chord, 125
midstay, 43, 57, 130
mildew, 114, 116
mizzen mast, 38, 55, 56
mizzens, 41, 56
mooring lines, 23–24, 35, 70
moorings:
  choice of, 28–29
  crew and, 78
  exposed, 29
  leaving of, 71–72
  picking up, 76–78
  securing boat in, 30–31
  tides and, 30, 31, 76, 77, 78
  wind and, 76, 77, 78

Narragansett Bay, 150, 153
National Advisory Committee for
  Aeronautics (NACA), 126
National Aeronautics and Space Administration (NASA), 181
National Oceanographic and Atmospheric
  Administration (NOAA), 177
Nautical Technologies Ltd., 121
naval pipe, 13, 15
navigation:
  area for, 4
  charts for, 4, 16, 60, 143–44, 156, 157, 164–70
  instruments for, 100, 109, 171, 177
  lights for, 15, 34
  log for, 144
navigation table, 4
navigator, 107, 144
netting, safety, 7–8
night vision, 104
non-skid surfaces, 4, 5

outboard motors, 10, 33, 34, 35, 39
outhaul, 135, 153
overboard, 178–82
Oxford Companion to Ships and the Sea, The
  (Kemp), 14